MANAGING THE UNTHINKABLE

The Role of Management in Challenging Times

D. Atif

iUniverse, Inc.
New York   Bloomington

Managing the Unthinkable
The Role of Management in Challenging Times

iUniverse books may be ordered through booksellers or by contacting:

iUniverse
1663 Liberty Drive
Bloomington, IN 47403
www.iuniverse.com
1-800-Authors (1-800-288-4677)

ISBN: 978-1-4401-4312-0 (pbk)
ISBN: 978-1-4401-4313-7 (ebook)

Printed in the United States of America

iUniverse rev. date: 10/8/2009

Dedicated to the Canadian Soldiers

Contents

INTRODUCTION

This book endeavors to take into account the gigantic real life day to day challenges managers face and provide a commonsense solution to challenges of management in recessionary times. Experts agree that the recession of 2008/2009 will be remembered if not for centuries at least for decades. In the midst of this historic macro economic meltdown there are managers who want to be doing the right thing by their constituents, subordinates and customers alike, but sometimes in the chaos of the moment they lose sight of what the right thing is. This book is an attempt at providing them with an armory of ideas and tested solutions to challenging situations that they can call upon when the going gets rough.

These are times when it is imperative for all of us to carry our load of responsibility within an organization. Unfortunately some employees use the macro-economic environment as an excuse not to deliver on what is expected of them but worse than that they look at the environment and use it as a psychological impediment to their own success. In these circumstances managers need to be equipped to clarify expectations, detail consequences of ignoring goals, know how to criticize respectfully and deal with mistakes.

In Communication loudness has been confused with toughness by managers for a long time. Stubbornness has been likened to superior understanding. Argumentativeness has been likened to honesty. I take a closer look at the road blocks to effective communication and how to negotiate them. I take a look at the role of feelings in communication. I pay great attention to the role of listening as an active, impactful skill in the process of communication. I discuss in detail how to offer feedback that is productive, respectful and actionable.

In these difficult times, perhaps the most challenging job for a manager is to create a positive mental attitude around the organization. The manager has to endeavor to create an environment of harmony, courage and success. It is the manager who has to create an environment in these times to create leaders around him and throughout the organization. Energy and enthusiasm are an essential part of a success oriented organization. It is up to the manager to create an environment that nurtures energy and enthusiasm. The manager also has the duty to create a culture of success that is unique and conducive to creating leaders all through the organization.

Another aspect that is exceptionally important to the success of an organization in these challenging times is the ability of the manager to set goals in a clear, tangible, realistic manner. As Harvey Mackay said a goal is a dream with a deadline. I present a guide to setting that deadline and achieving it.

For a manager, managing external elements within an organization is important but the most important and, in my opinion, the most neglected part of the organization is management of self. Without it, managers may do more harm than good. Just as incompetent doctors, incompetent managers may make people, figuratively, sicker and less vital. A great degree of self-awareness is necessary for a successful manager. One's capacity to align words and deeds depends on how well one knows herself. The better one knows oneself, the better one can make sense of the often incomprehensible and conflicting messages one receives daily. We need internal guidance to navigate the permanent white waters of today's environment.

I discuss self-confidence here. It is not the same as competence, of course. Knowing that you have the competence and believing that in a given situation you can use your skills to achieve your goals are different mental functions.

Beliefs about one's capabilities influence personal motivation. They determine how much effort a person is likely to exert and how long the individual will persevere when the task gets difficult. The greater the self-efficacy, the less stress and depression people feel in taxing and threatening situations. The greater the belief in their own capabilities the higher the goals people set for themselves and the firmer they are in commitment to them.

Here I also touch upon ways in which a manager can increase discipline in himself and develop a complete understanding of his own strengths and weaknesses. I touch upon ways in which a manger can build character based on personal and corporate values. I also endeavor to develop an innate audit for ability to succeed.

The passionate search for opportunities beyond what is the status quo comes with a certain degree of risk. It requires creativity, innovation and more than all else guts.

Good managers are open to stepping into untested waters and accepting the risks that accompany all experiments. The first step is emancipating one's self of psychologically self-imposed limitations. Innovation is imperative to the healthy growth of the organization. Without constant innovation in products and services an organization will plateau. We need to look outside the existing way of doing things if we're to be innovative. Here a manager who is respectful of the past but is confident enough to take the plunge into the unpredictable without caring about other people's opinions triumphs.

A little bit of a 'do not care' attitude is essential because an integral part of risk taking is that the manager puts himself and others at risk. In fact not only that he takes risks himself but also encourages others to take risks as well. In fact one of the most glaring differences between the manager and the bureaucrat is the good manager's inclination to encourage risk taking, to encourage others to step out into the unknown rather than to play it safe. He builds risk taking into the goal setting process. He sets goals that are higher than current levels, but not so high that people feel only frustration and are so burnt by the risk taking process that they are too shy to try again. Managers raise the bar gradually and offer coaching and training to build skills that help people get over each new level of risk taking. I discuss the ability to take risks as an essential trait of a successful manager.

There is no simple method for determining the appropriate level of risk in a project. We must weigh pros and cons, costs and benefits, potential losses versus potential gains. Realizing that one person's challenge is another's routine activity, we must factor in the present skill levels of the team members and the demands of the task. But even if we could compute risk to a negligible level, every innovation would still expose us to some uncertainty. Perhaps the healthiest thing we can do is evaluate whether what we can learn is worth the cost. And our ability to grow and learn under stressful, risk-abundant situations is highly based on how we respond to change.

A special trait of the great manager is a substantial tolerance for failure. James Burke, Johnson & Johnson's CEO, says one of J&J's tenets is that "you've got to be willing to fail." Emerson Charles Knight argues: "You need the ability to fail. You cannot innovate unless you are willing to accept mistakes." Tolerance for failure is a very specific part of the excellent company culture – and that lesson comes directly from the top. Constituents have to make lots of tries and consequently suffer some failures or the organization won't learn and grow.

Reengineering, re-strategizing, mergers, downsizing, quality efforts, and cultural renewal projects have become an integral part of business today in North America. Powerful flat-world economic forces are at work here, and these forces may grow even stronger over the next few decades. As a result, more and more organizations will be pushed to reduce costs, improve the quality of products and services, locate new opportunities for growth, and increase productivity. The twenty-first-century employee will need to know more about both leadership and management than did his or her twentieth century counterpart. Without these skills charismatic adaptive enterprises will not be possible.

Managers want to change the organization, overcoming obstacles to their vision, and that means overcoming inner vulnerabilities, adapting new skills, and adhering to new values. The challenge for business leaders is to be a combination of warrior and prophet, delivering high performance in the business and being an advocate for their vision of the organization. Business has to continually change in small ways to stay competitive and may have to change drastically in response to external conditions.

The rate of change in the business world is not going to slow down anytime soon. If anything, competition in most industries will probably speed up over the next few decades. Enterprises everywhere will be presented with even more terrible hazards and wonderful opportunities, driven by the challenges faced of the economy along with related technological and social trends.

To date, major change efforts have helped some organizations adapt significantly to shifting conditions, have improved the competitive standing of others, and have positioned a few for a far better future. But in too many situations the improvements have been negligible and many organizations have failed to understand that change is essential. The options are either to grow or to shrink. They cannot afford to celebrate their achievements of the past and rest on their laurels. If they resist change the result would be wasted resources.

COMMUNICATING AS A MANAGER

The Impact of Powerful Communication

Communication is the basis of all business. The ability to commune well is what lights the fire in employees. It's what turns great proposals into action. It's what makes all accomplishment possible. On the other hand, an indisposition to listen that is common in managers can cost the company a lot. A bulk of all management setbacks are the result of defective communication. In Communication loudness has been confused with toughness by managers. Stubbornness has been likened to superior understanding. Argumentativeness has been likened to honesty. Communication is connecting.

If you have seen a colony of ants working, you have seen some astonishing linking in. Ants are impressive because individually they have limited intelligence and yet together they are champions of teamwork. Their engineering deftness that requires considerable cooperation is sophisticated. Underground nests are planned to have abundant supply of oxygen, and the mound on top is engineered to adjust the nest's temperature. When temperatures fall, the ants are mobilized to obstruct the openings with dirt; if conditions become too desiccated, members of the settlement go out to find water and fetch it back to increase the humidity. Ants work together to solve predicaments. How can they be so resourceful and efficient? An important strength may be that they are not capable of miscommunication. It is believed that they communicate messages chemically through antennae hormone trails on the ground. Therefore they get information in its most unadulterated form. No past experiences, assumptions or suppositions get in the way. There is no hurried or slapdash communication causing confusion or uncertainty. If only most businesses could learn from them.

Human teams don't quite function as well as some of the other species when it comes to communication. Information sent and received is never pure within a team setting. It has been tainted by personal experience, assessed by our beliefs and manipulated by the receiver's opinion of the sender. The greater the contamination of the ideas shared, the less likely it is that the team can work seamlessly and synergistically. Often an insufficient amount of information is communed and it is communicated sloppily by people in a hurry.

Perhaps the most potent principle of all human interaction: authentically seeking to understand another before being understood in return. At the root of most interpersonal troubles is failure to carefully understand each other. The actual disagreements of matter are magnified and compounded by the lack of ability to see the world not through another's eyes but through the person's heart and mind. We misinterpret and therefore mistrust motives, we are so ego-invested in promoting our own ideas, defending our stance, attacking opposing opinion, judging, evaluating, probing and challenging that we normally listen with the intention not to understand but retort.

Through empathic communication we get not only a lucid comprehension of another's needs, and ideas, but also assurance that we are actually understood as well. Genuine empathic communication shares authentically not only words, thoughts, and information, but also sentiments, emotions, and sensitivities. We are raised to believe that investing the time and energy to understand another deeply withholding judgment denotes agreement and support. This is not so but such patterns are hard to break. The pattern of seeking first to understand is crucial to maximizing quality. Effective communication between administration and labor, between the corporation and its suppliers, and between the customers and the company is essential to maximizing quality.

The Role of Feelings in Communication

Good managers move us. They stimulate passion in us and bring out our best. When we try to elucidate why they are so effective, vision, planning and powerful ideas come to mind. But the reality is much more basic: Good management works through the feelings. No matter what managers set out to do - whether it's charting a course of action or mobilizing teams - their triumph depends on how they do it as much as it does on what they do. Even if they get everything else right, if leaders fail in this task of driving feelings in the right direction, nothing will work as well as it could.

Feelings are often seen as too personal or unquantifiable to talk about in a meaningful way. But research in the field of feelings has capitulated keen insights into not only how to quantify the impact of a manager's emotions but also how good managers have found efficient ways to understand and advance the way they handle their own and employees' emotions. Understanding the potent role of feelings in the workplace sets the top managers apart from the rest - not just in tangibles such as better revenue results and the retention of talented individuals but also in the key intangibles, such as higher morale, enthusiasm, and dedication.

The reason a manager's manner matters so much lies in the blueprint of the human brain where the emotional centers rely mostly upon resources outside of our selves. We rely on connections with other people for our own emotional balance. Research in intensive care wards has shown that the presence of another human being not only lowers the patient's blood pressure, but also slows the discharge of fatty acids that block arteries. Whereas three or more incidents of severe stress within one year triple the death rate in socially isolated older people, they have no impact whatsoever on the death rate of people who cultivate many close relationships.

Being able to pick up on emotional hints is particularly significant in situations where people have reasons to hide their true feelings - a fact of life in the corporate world. Sensing what the feelings of others are without their saying so captures the spirit of empathy. Others hardly ever tell us in words what they feel; instead they tell us in their tone, expressions, or non-verbal body language.

The key to knowing others' emotional topography is a familiarity with our own. However, highly attuned understanding demands we put aside our emotional agendas for the moment so that we can lucidly receive the other person's signals. When we are entangled in our own strong feelings, we are off on a dissimilar physiological tangent, unreceptive to the more subtle signals that allow connection.

Charles Darwin suggested that the ability to interpret feelings has played a huge role in human evolution, both in creating and maintaining the social order. In evolution, negative feelings - fear and rage - had enormous survival value, driving a terrorized animal to fight or flee. In a way this evolutionary leftover is still with us today; during our own anxiety causing interfaces, we respond more strongly to someone in a bad mood than to someone in a good one. This can be a formula for emotional devastation, creating a feedback loop of negativity or anger.

The precondition for gaining the capability to measure the other person's feelings is self-awareness. Among managers the most effective are able to tune into their own indications for emotions - an essential for any job where understanding matters.

Our nervous system is involuntarily set to engage in this emotional empathy. But how effectively we use this capability is for the most part a learned ability that depends on motivation. People who have lived in extreme social seclusion are poor at reading emotional signs in those around them not because they lack the essential circuitry for empathy but because they have never learned to pay attention to these messages and so have not practiced this ability.

Scientists have captured the attunement of feelings by measuring the heart rate of two people as they have a pleasant tête-à-tête. As the conversation commences their bodies each operate at dissimilar levels of heart rate. But by the end of a simple fifteen-minute chat, their physiological profiles seem astonishingly similar - a phenomenon called mirroring. This occurs even more strongly during the descending spiral of a conflict, when rage and hurt reverberate. It is seen again and again how feelings spread irresistibly in this manner whenever people are near one another, even when the contact is absolutely non-verbal.

When two people start to speak with each other, they begin to fall into a delicate dance of rhythmic accord, synchronizing their actions and postures, their verbal pitch, and even the length of pauses between one individual's speaking and the other's response. This mutual imitation goes on subconsciously, and seems to be directed by the most primitive areas of the brain. These instruments kick in with spectacular rapidity, as quickly as a tenth of a second. When this routine coordination is missing, we feel a little uncomfortable. In sixty work teams across various industries members who sat in meetings together ended up sharing moods within about two hours.

Communicating With the Boss

It is the manager who contributes the most to the emotional atmosphere. Because of that lasting truth of business that everyone watches the boss. Employees take their emotional prompts from the top. Even when the CEO works at the other side of closed doors his manner affects the feelings of his direct reports, and a domino effect ripples through the company's environment. Examination of working teams in action revealed numerous ways the manager plays such a crucial role in determining the communal emotions. Managers typically talked more than everyone else and more attention was paid to what they said. Managers were usually the first to speak out on a subject, and when others made comments, their remarks were often referred to what the manager had said than to anyone else's comments. Because the manager's way of seeing things has special weight, managers direct meaning for a group, offering a way to construe, and so react emotionally to a situation.

But the impact on the emotional environment in the organization goes beyond what a manager says. Even when managers are not talking, they are watched more carefully than everyone else in the group. Indeed, employees often see the manager's reaction as the most legitimate response, and so model their own on it - especially in a circumstance they have not been faced with before and where various employees react differently. In a sense, the manager sets the emotional standard.

Managers give praise or hold back, criticize well or unsympathetically, offer support or take no notice of employees' needs. They can structure the team's mission in ways that give meaning to each employee's contribution – or not. They can steer in ways that give people a sense of lucidity and purpose in their work. They have the capability to allow people to use their best sense of how to get the job done.

How successful a manager is in refining the organization's emotional climate, has to do with how expressively his face, voice and gestures convey his emotions. If you think about the managers with whom people most want to work in an organization, they have this ability to exude positive feelings. It is the one reason emotionally sensitive managers attract accomplished people - for the pleasure of working in their presence. On the contrary, managers who emit the negative energy, domineering, cold or outright ruthless - repel people. No one wants to work for a grump. Optimistic, zealous, positive leaders more easily retain their people, compared with managers who tend toward negative moods.

Although all this talk of feelings and moods may seem frivolous from a business viewpoint, they have real consequences for accomplishing organizational objectives. A manager's mild unease can act as a signal that something needs more and urgent attention. However, managers should be careful while exhibiting anxiety as mild anxiety can focus attention and energy but prolonged distress can sabotage a manager's relationships and also hinder work performance by reducing the brain's ability to process information and respond effectively. Of all the interactions at most companies that pitch employees into bad moods, the most frequent were talking to someone in management. Interactions with managers led to frustration, disappointment or anger. These interactions are cause of distress more often than customers, work pressure, company policies or personal problems. An upbeat mood, on the other hand, more often enhances the neural abilities crucial for doing good work. Not that managers need to be overly "nice"; the art of good management includes pressing the reality of work demands without overly upsetting people. One of the established laws of psychology holds that beyond a moderate level, increases in anxiety and worry erode mental capabilities. The number of times people feel positive emotions at work turns out to be one of the strongest forecasters of satisfaction, and therefore, for instance, of how likely employees are to quit.

When people feel good, they perform at their best. Feeling good lubricates mental effectiveness, making people better at comprehending information. Upbeat moods, make people view others - or events - in a more positive light. That helps people feel more positive about their ability to achieve a goal, enhances creativity and decision making skills, and prompts people to be helpful. Sales executives with a glass-is-half-full outlook, for example, are far more able than their more pessimistic peers to persist in spite of rejections, so they generate more business opportunities. Moreover, research on humor at work reveals that a timely joke or lighthearted laughter can inspire creativity, open lines of communication and trust. Playful humor increases the likelihood of financial concessions during a negotiation. No wonder then that playfulness holds a prominent place in the tool kit of good managers.

Good moods are especially important when it comes to teams: The ability of a manager to pitch a team into a keen, cooperative mood can determine its success. On the other hand, whenever emotional clashes in a team sap attention and energy from their shared tasks, a team's performance will suffer.

Communicating and sharing information is a significant determinant in building up employees' capacity. Instead of closeting a small group of key executives to develop a strategy based upon the manager's own agenda, the manager should hold a series of meetings over several days and allow a larger group to develop and help choose alternatives. As a result of having been involved in the process all team members know what to do and why.

Managers understand that unless they communicate and share information with their employees, few will take much interest in what is going on. When managers share information rather than guard it, employees feel included and respected. A greater flow of information is created. When employees have the same information with common values and shared interests, the results flow. Finally, everyone can sing in harmony, from the same page of the same song sheet.

Roadblocks to Effective Communication

Unfortunately being unable to truly communicate is a lot easier than communicating effectively. So much so that berating and rebuking employees are widely accepted forms of interaction even inside some of the largest and best-known companies in the world. The right to talk down to employees is thought to be a natural privilege of executive positions.

When it comes to communicating most people do not listen with the intent to understand; they listen with the intent to reply. In corporate environments managers are either speaking or preparing to speak. They're filtering everything through their own prototypes, reading their biography into their employees' situations.

Often miscommunication is the result of conjectures. A good manager never lets a hypothesis slip without challenging it. But the greatest danger comes from the assumptions that remain unspoken for they are most likely to prevent team members from connecting. One of the most precarious assumptions one can make as a manager that we have been heard and understood. We know that a teenager saying "Sure okay" as he runs out the door is no proof that he actually heard the instructions.

Perception problems may eventually grow to become personality conflicts. Trustworthiness problems are far more difficult to resolve, primarily because each of the employees thinks he sees the world as it is rather than as he is. Unaware of the deformation in his own perception, his attitude is: "If you disagree with me, in my eyes you are wrong, simply because I am sure that I am right."

Whenever we are so sure of our being right as to make everyone who thinks differently feel wrong, their best protection from further injury from us is to label us and to put us behind mental bars for an indefinite jail sentence, and we will not be released until we pay the highest price. Most such personality conflicts in work environments can be resolved if one or both of the parties involved will realize that at the root is a perception problem.

Listening

Listening is the most important of all communication skills. It is more important than stimulating speechifying, more important than an authoritative voice and more important than talent for the written word.

True listening involves much more than understanding the words that are said, it involves sharing another person's point of view. In fact only 10 percent of our communication is represented by the words we say. Another 30 percent is represented by our sound and

60 percent by our body language. In true listening, you listen with your ears but you also listen with your eyes and heart. You listen for sentiment, for purpose. You listen for mannerism. You use your right brain in addition to your left. You sense, you discern.

True listening is so potent because instead of assigning your own life story, you attempt to get inside another person's head and heart. You're listening to understand. You are trying to learn what is important to the person you are trying to make an impact on, because nothing you do can impress unless the other person perceives it as such. You can try as much as you possibly can to impress only to have it turn into nothing when a person regards your labors as manipulative or self-serving because you don't recognize what really matters to him or her.

Paying full attention and trying to rise above one's autobiography, and seeking to see things from another's point of view takes valor and internal sources of security. It means being open to new knowledge and to change. That is listening.

When you listen with attention to an employee you give him or her psychological validation and after that essential need is met you can then focus on influencing or problem solving. A fact of life is that satisfied desires do not inspire. It's the unsatisfied needs that motivate. Next to physical survival, the greatest requirement of a human being is psychological survival - to be affirmed, validated and appreciated.

An inability to listen can be injurious to the internal environment of the organization. For instance, uncovering the emotional hub of an organization is the manager's task. But too many managers fail to listen to the truth, which can leave them prey to being out of touch. They can never inspire employees because they never listen to what inspires them. In their most gentle form such managers seem to have no time for important conversations, and do not build the kind of relationships that result in deep discourse about what is important to their employees and what is not. They don't have enough real contact with employees in their organizations to get a sense of what is going on, living in a kind of obscure air that leaves them out of touch with the underlying emotional reality of daily life. Less benign are managers who use severe methods and actually prevent employees from telling them what is important to them.

An inability to listen is at the base of the manager taking too much responsibility himself and micromanaging. Listening is the first step towards empowerment. The most active change the manager may have to make in order to grant empowerment to the staff members is to truly listen to their opinions and their concerns. The good manager has to acknowledge that employees are intelligent and perceptive and that he cannot make up his mind on what action should be taken until the employee makes a case for his or her own plan. Even when you believe that you intuitively know what to do, your job is now to help your employees learn how to solve their own problems. You can do this by coaching yourself to allow them to do their own problem solving and trying to limit your contribution to supervision and advice. You can then turn your mind to higher-level matters rather than micromanaging.

An inability to listen can be equally costly in external relationships for an organization. When a salesperson is anxious to make a sale he does not listen as well. He loses invaluable opportunities to tailor the solutions being provided or building credibility by acknowledging a valid objection or presenting a feature as a benefit.

In sales and business development circles some see empathy quite negatively, contending that taking the customer's point of view will affect negatively sales of products or services customers don't really want or need. This of course, implies a somewhat skeptical view of the salesperson's task, as though it is only about making the sale, not developing a relationship with the customer. It also presumes the potential customer to be a passive and naïve individual almost coerced into making the purchase.

A more progressive view of sales, though, sees the task as being able to listen well and understand what the customer or client needs, and then finding a method to meet those needs. The old stereotype that sales go to the fast-talking extrovert does not hold up in today's intricate business world. Buyers today favor the reps who are most empathic and who care about their needs and concerns. The foundation of empathy is a profound understanding of the buyer's point of view.

Creating a composed receptive environment is where good listening begins. It is very difficult to ever listen effectively when angst or anxiety is present. That's why good managers always make sure their environs are comfortable, hospitable places.

Effectual listening requires an avid involvement in a conversation, even when the listener's lips are still. It takes focus. It requires authentic engagement. It demands some kind of response brisk, thoughtful and on target. It must follow closely with what was just said. Nonetheless, I do not mean to suggest interrupting the other person every ten words. Effective listeners become skilled at a few techniques of listening that they find comfortable and natural and remember to put them to work. It can be an intermittent nod, or I see. Some people smile or shake their heads. Strong eye contact is another way of indicating, "Yes, I am listening to what you are telling me."

What's imperative here isn't the precise listening technique that is chosen. None of these methods should ever be used in a taut or stiff way.

The important thing is to listen before you start talking away and telling everybody how smart you are. If you disagree with them you may be tempted to butt in. But do not. They won't pay attention while they still have a lot of ideas of theirs crying for expression. So listen patiently and with an open mind. Be sincere about it. Encourage them to express their ideas fully. Listen very intently, and don't make up your mind too quickly.

It is astounding how rare effective communication is considering we have all been communicating almost all of our lives. The greatest mistake managers make besides thinking they are the greatest source of all wisdom is failing to appreciate that communication absolutely must be a two-way street. As a manager you have to share your ideas and listen to the ideas of your employees with earnestness and focus. If you can show your employees you are receptive to their ideas, they are more likely to be amenable to yours. And if you have the patience to pay attention to the many ideas that are mediocre you won't miss out on that one great one from an employee.

It is easy to become detached from customers and colleagues as you rise in an organization. However, no matter how high you get, communication still has to run in all directions, talking and listening.

Story Telling as Effective Communication

Managers who create and tell engaging human stories are better communicators than those who can't or don't. The ability to tell certain kinds of dramatic stories, and align them with the point at hand, is not only a useful tool but also an essential weapon in the struggle to communicate. It is so effective to use stories because we never outgrow our child-like feelings for stories where we identify with the characters.

There are two basic types of stories that managers use to engage and energize employees. The first of these are personal stories. Managers use these stories to describe their primary views about the world and to explain how they developed those views. These stories serve as vehicles to both communicate the manager's views and build an understanding between the manager and his or her employees.

The second type of stories is that which communes the vision of the manager. Management is about change, about taking an organization or a group of people from where they are now to where they need to be. And the best way to get employees to venture into unknown territory is to make that terrain familiar and desirable by taking them there first in their imaginations. Good managers create and use future stories to help people break away from the familiar present and venture boldly ahead to create a better future. They not only describe the future in terms that are personal and compelling, but they help others understand why and what they must do to get there. Without being able to do that, would-be leaders never get the sustained effort required to move toward their goal.

Quantity of Communication

In teams that have a deliberate direction and are heading there with energy and enthusiasm the manager takes every opportunity to communicate with the team members and in each conversation passionately keeps the ultimate vision in front of them. But it is not a onetime thing. Keeping the level of enthusiasm high requires constant stoking of the fire on the part of the manager.

In an annual ranking of Canada's top employer's by Report on Business magazine and Hewitt Associates, it was noted in 2002 that, on average, CEOs at the 50 best companies spent 4 days a month with staff. That's 48 days a year, a big piece of any manager's work year.

But the most potent conversations are not formal, structured events. They are the spontaneous chats that managers pepper their team with every time they get a chance. The good manager talks about the unlimited possibilities even in dire present circumstances. Talk about what makes his team or organization extraordinary. What people often take greatest pride in is how their team and organization does what they do and what they believe in.

Although the message must be repeated but it need not be so detailed that it takes a lot of the manager's time. In fact, managers who most successfully motivate people have boiled their key message down to a few words. One might think of those words as a mantra. Lou Gerstner, when working to turn IBM around, realized that although he talked about core values all the time and the messages was getting through it had been received only at an intellectual level. He boiled it down to three words: Win, Execute and Team.

The Meeting Game

In the field of corporate communications the significance of meetings is grossly underestimated. A large part of the important decisions are made in meetings.

Meetings have a bit of a bad reputation in spite of their importance perhaps because too often they are a mere simulation of the forceful process they are intended to be. Everyone has likely experienced meetings that accomplished little or nothing, in which there was an inability to reach consensus, or had a meeting leader who drove the meeting with little appreciation of team members' input.

According to Pace Productivity Research, front-line workers expend, on average 6.5 hours per week or 14 per cent of their time in meetings. Managers expend 10 hours per week or 19 per cent of their time in meetings. No matter how frequent your meetings are if they are less efficient than they could be you are wasting precious people power. This waste is trivial compared to the other costs of ineffective meetings.

Meetings and efficient teamwork go hand in hand as part of setting the right tone within the organization. Effective meetings mean effective teams. Without meetings it's difficult, even impossible, for team members to have a common vision and goal, and a full understanding of the issues and of one another.

Therefore, no activity in the organizational culture affects results more directly than meetings. Meetings can generate synergy. The effectiveness of a meeting affects the quality of the decisions that come out of it and the degree of support the decisions get. The right decisions and fervent support for them are the factors that most determine the quality of your results.

Every team's development plan should include honing meeting facilitating skills. Hence establishing meeting ground rules and agreements in the beginning is a very effective method and the most potent tool a leader has. They offer the fastest way to improve meetings and their outcomes and are the first step in creating the right atmosphere where members connect powerfully with one another.

Some ground rules can be pretty straightforward and obvious and one might think that it is not worth putting down on paper in an agreement form like no one being allowed to interrupt or shout down another team member's contribution during the meeting. Yet, it is astonishing how minor things like this put in writing provide structure and legitimacy to organizational meetings. If there is one place in the managerial culture where being specific about minor details and laying down expectations of the employees explicitly upfront is vital it is in this process of establishing and enforcing meeting ground rules and agreements.

Another effective tool that the good manager has in his armor to orchestrate efficient meetings is the agenda. It can help the manager plan and manage the meeting and help participants prepare for the meeting and evaluate its success after the meeting.

Feedback

With comprehensive feedback that includes factors like quality, capacity, suitability, and relationship management people can become self-corrective and can more easily comprehend the role they play in the grand scheme of things. With feedback they can also find out what help they need.

In those cases where performance has lagged behind expectations and feedback does not comprise of good news the feedback process can be discouraging. However, it depends upon people's conviction in their capacities. Those who distrust their abilities are easily discouraged. Those who have confidence in themselves and the person providing the feedback increase their efforts when their performance falls short. They persevere until they succeed. Hence, there is all the more reason to build people's capability and confidence and to create an environment in which they can assume responsibility.

Communication and feedback are at the core of the management process. The best way to run an organization is to make certain that everyone knows the tenets of the game; that is how the organization makes money and generates income. At most organizations, no one explains how one person's actions affect another's, how each department depends on the others, what impact they all have on the organization as a whole. So people should be taught the rules and shown how to quantify effectiveness and follow the action but also elucidated the impact of their actions if they drop the ball.

There is no denying the negative connotations we associate with getting Feedback. It is true that benefits we can derive from Feedback are lost in the dynamics of power that have infiltrated the feedback process and the notion of feedback is equated with being judged, criticized or even being attacked by another, usually of higher status. Although there is much discomfort around the notion of feedback leading to reluctance to provide it, it seems that if employees don't get it, they will infer it for themselves, with all the hazards that entails. Although the tendency to self-assess in itself may not be concerning, and in fact is important, the assumptions made may well be quite off the mark.

So the process of the presentation of feedback is important. Rather than it being presented as criticism, disapproval or a personal attack feedback should be presented as information and not judgment. With a realization that it is hard to keep a non-defensive and open attitude to another's assessment of our actions. Because a major part of our self-image is based on how others view us, it can be hard to open up to re-examination. We might have to explain to employees that the feedback someone provides is his perception of the interaction or event and not reality per se, it frees them to move beyond a position where they feel judged and criticized. Another important factor to remember is that if, after careful consideration, the feedback seems off the mark, it may be because the feedback says more about the person delivering it than it does about the receiver.

Relationships: The Crucial Dimension

The crucial factor in communication is the relationship. Many niggling knots develop in communication lines due to interpersonal relations. When relationships are strained, we must be careful about the words we use or we risk being misunderstood. When relationships are strained, people become apprehensive and distrustful, refusing to interpret the intent of the words.

On the other hand when the relationship is harmonious we can nearly communicate without words. When the relationship is not well established, a book

D. Atif

full of words won't be enough to communicate meaning because meanings are not found in words - they are found in people. That's the case with so many of us. We want to be understood without accepting the other person's point of view. Our dialogues become collective monologues, and we never truly understand what is going on inside another human being's mind.

In a management position telling people they ought to have known what you meant or they should have understood what you wanted them to do is an instant recipe for disaster. People should not be expected to be psychics. Nor should they have to decode what you want by having to go through a maze of subtle clues.

Many misunderstandings occur in this manner. You assume that employees know what you're thinking and when their actions reveal otherwise, your first reaction is to blame them. You assume that somehow employees are on the same wavelength as you, even if their actions consistently tell you they are not. If people are persistently misunderstanding your messages, odds are that you are not communicating very well. A manager who was a champion of clarity when it came to communication was Jack Welch. Whenever he was being briefed by employees he would challenge them to explain to him as if "he was a two year old". This kind of humility is not only charming it is also extremely productive since inherently there is a hesitance in the corporate culture today to demand clarity because an idea or concept was too multifarious.

Overpromising and under-delivering

One also has to be careful not to over-promise the

employees one manages. Over promising is a trap into which it's very easy to fall. Let's say an employee comes in to see you. They want a raise or a promotion. It's natural to want to mollify them, to make that employee feel hopeful. So you give them the hint of a promise. Not a genuine promise etched in stone, but the hope of a promise. You somewhat hang it out there; you say something vague in the vein of, 'I'll see what I can do."

But what happens is that employee leaves your office and you basically forget about it. After all, you are having this sort of conversations all the time. And you haven't in fact promised them anything so what's to remember? But, that person remembers.

Even though you did not intend to, you have led that employee on, given him or her hope that that promotion or raise is just around the corner if he or she keeps at it.

Promising something raises an employee's hopes and when those hopes are not delivered that person is going to rail against you. He is going to believe that you lied to him, deceived him in some way. Now you might be completely innocent in all this. But you have gotten yourself into a corner by either promising too much, or suggesting a promise of what you cannot deliver. So be careful what you promise and write down what you promise.

It's a basic fact about communicating with employees: they would not say what they think - and would not listen receptively to what you say - unless a basis of authentic trust and common interest has been laid. You can't be insincere. How you really feel about communication, whether you are open or not, comes through loud and clear, no matter what you say.

There is no trick to it. Well, that is not entirely true. There is. You can make sure that you communicate better. It is by being open, liking employees and letting them know you do. Being down-to-earth and modest and believing that everyone's the same, whether you are the CEO of a company or a salesperson. It's just another job. That's what creating a receptive atmosphere is about: putting people at ease.

Once people do take the chance of telling you what they think, don't penalize them for their openness. Do absolutely nothing to dispirit them from taking the risk of communicating again.

The key to communication is the relationship. The moment we enter into this special relationship with an employee we begin to change the nature of our communication with them. We begin to build faith and confidence in each other. In this context mull over the value of a private visit with each employee, a lunch with a business associate, a chat with a client or customer - a time when your attention is centered upon that person, upon his or her interests, apprehensions, needs, hopes and fears.

To listen truly to another on serious issues takes a colossal amount of internal personal security. It exposes the vulnerabilities in us. We may be impacted and changed but if down deep we are feeling insecure, we can't afford to risk being changed. We need a sense of predictability. That is the composition of prejudice. We judge and shape an opinion beforehand. The specter of change petrifies most of us.

If we are influenced as a consequence of vigilant listening, we need to be able to feel solid and appreciate that our core character is uninterrupted.

To be effective in presenting your viewpoint, start by demonstrating a vivid understanding of the alternative points of view. Advocate them better than their sponsors can. Doing that robs your opponents of the chance to resist you; they have to partake in the solution.

Taking other people's perspectives into consideration requires significant thought and practice. But the effort pays off, mainly in environments where building and maintaining long-term relationships is deemed more valuable than realizing short-term gains. This is especially true in the case of organizations that depend on internal and external tactical alliances and are in the practice of selling high value products or services.

Questions To Ask

1) Do you remain quiet to allow someone to finish speaking even though you disagree with what you hear? Do you hold your emotions in check as well?

2) Do you listen between the lines, looking for hidden meanings and watching body language, to determine what the person is really saying?

3) Do you paraphrase to ensure that you have not misunderstood what has been said?

4) Do you set up meetings so you won't be distracted?

5) When some member of your staff wants to speak to you, do you clear your desk and your mind to give the individual your full attention?

6) If you can't pull yourself away from what you are doing, do you set up a time to meet with the staff members to give him or her your full attention?

7) Are you receptive to other Colleagues' ideas?

8) Do you think berating people is a right of the boss?

9) Can you sense what other people feel without them saying it?

10) Do your constituents sometimes incorrectly make assumptions about your message?

11) Do you ever over promise or make statements that can be assumed to be promises?

12) Do you use analogies a lot and make your point by telling stories?

13) Do the meetings you hold contribute to the organizational effectiveness?

14) Do your constituents find the feedback you give to be useful?

15) Are you sensitive to constituents' body language in the communication process?

Creating A Positive Mental Attitude

The Inherent Tensions and Contradictions

There is an intrinsic tension for employees in organizations between what they would want to do and the restrictions enforced upon them by the organization. This tension in the workplace can potentially be disastrous if left unchecked.

Examples of these contradictions within an organization for employees might include when do they surrender to another's authority, and when do they fight back against it? When do they set perimeters, and when do they break the rules? When do they elect to listen and when do they tell?

To say that managers should always enhance individual freedom within the organization and let all rules slide is rather unrealistic. To say that employees should always accept the rules and never defy them is equally unrealistic. We can count on people to strive to be as free as possible and we can also count on organizations to exert restrictions. Part of a manager's job is to engage employees in dealing with the strain between freedom and constraint.

This struggle is noticed in experiments with time off, in-company day care, parental leave, etc. Managers are experimenting with these and many other strategies to create a positive mental attitude amongst employees. There is a continuous dialogue between free will and restraint. More autonomy is becoming less of an exception but it would be foolish to expect organizations to dump all rules and constraints. Institutions must have perimeters; the question is not whether these exist, but how many, how much, and what type. And most importantly, are these restrictions a product of someone's personal insecurities or are they truly in the best interest of the organization.

Employees expect their managers to have a clear vision for the future of the organization. Employees also expect managers to be inspiring – to be energetic and positive. Managers must be able to communicate their vision in ways that motivate and encourage employees to enlist.

Another contradiction within the ranks of employees is that being imaginative and being exciting is often not harmonious with being cooperative and dependable. If your vision of the future is opposed to that of your superiors, you may be perceived as disloyal even if your view is more effective for the organization. Persistently offering a point of view may only reinforce this perception and may reduce the support of colleagues and managers alike.

There is a critical difference between a farsighted leader and a trustworthy colleague. Though success in both is founded on individual credibility, leadership requires the realization of an exclusive and ideal image of the future. Teamwork requires collaboration and consistent adherence to that common vision. Leadership and teamwork are certainly not mutually exclusive – in fact, an exemplary manager fosters collaboration – yet there is a dynamic tension between them.

However, if individuals cannot be taught to subordinate themselves to a shared intention, then no one will follow and anarchy will rule. And yet in order to grow and improve, organizations must create a climate that stimulates leadership; they must encourage the sincere articulation of new strategic visions of the future.

In these tentative times of business transformation it is completely necessary for executives to promote and put up with more internal conflict than has been permitted in the past. If organizations expect employees to show initiative in meeting today's business challenges, then they have to relax their expectations of devotion. Instead they must support efforts of competent people to find answers to the problems that their companies are faced with. In short, they must develop the manager in every employee and, at the same time, keep them disciplined.

Importance of the Environment and Impact of the Manager

In the face of these intrinsic contradictions, we require the manager to create a positive mental attitude within an organization. Most companies don't fail because they are wrong; most fail because they don't commit themselves. They squander away their momentum and their priceless resources while attempting to make a decision. The greatest peril is standing still. When a company is meandering its staff is demoralized and every employee feels paralyzed. This is precisely when you need to have a strong manager setting a direction. And it does not even have to be the best direction – just a firm, clear one. After the course is set, the manager has to create a positive environment for his employees to work in.

Good managers are very aware of the strength the employees hold in their brains. The way one thought or feeling can dramatically change the situation. They know that what they think defines them. Outside influences can determine individual happiness to a very limited degree the rest is their own psychological outlook and intrinsic mental strength. What matters is the way they react to those influences, well or badly. To develop that sort of approach, to make their constituents proactive rather than reactive is the main concern. They train their employees to anticipate consequences. They make them cognizant of it every day. They train them to become results-oriented but also make them value and take pleasure in the journey. The message there being that satisfaction is more a mode of traveling than the destination they are traveling to.

If we consider the results of a study of fifty CEOs of the leading Canadian service companies such as consulting and accounting firms, not-for-profit organizations, and government agencies. The CEOs and their top management team members were assessed on how energetic, enthusiastic and determined they were. They were also asked how much conflict and tumult the top team experienced, that is, personality clashes, anger and friction in meetings, and emotional conflicts in contrast to disagreement about ideas.

The study found that the more positive the moods of people in the top management team, the more co-operatively they functioned and the better the company's business results. Put differently, the longer a business was run by a management team that did not get along, the shoddier the company's market return.

Common wisdom holds that employees who feel upbeat will go the extra mile to gratify customers and therefore improve the bottom line. There is a logarithm that predicts that relationship: For every 1 percent enhancement in the service climate, there's a 2 percent boost in revenue.

Benjamin Schneider, a University of Maryland professor, found in operations as sundry as bank branches, insurance companies, call centers, and hospitals that employees' rating of service atmosphere predicted customer satisfaction, which drove business results. Similarly, poor morale among customer service reps at a given point in time predicts turnover - and declining customer satisfaction - up to three years later. This low customer satisfaction then contributes to declining revenues.

So the answer then is that besides the obvious relationships between climate and working conditions or salary, good managers play a key role. In general, the more demanding the work, the more empathic and supportive the manager needs to be. Managers drive the service climate and thus the tendency of employees to satisfy customers. At an insurance company for instance, Schneider found that effective management influenced service climate among agents to account for up to 4 percent difference in insurance renewals - a seemingly minute margin that made a significant difference to the business.

The factors deciding which organizations prove most fit in any given quarter are scandalously complex. But analysis suggests that, all in all, the climate - how people feel about working at an organization — may account for 20 to 30 percent of business performance. Creating a comfortable environment for employees pays off in hard results.

If climate drives business results, what drives climate? Roughly 50 to 70 percent of how employees perceive their organization's climate can be traced to the actions of one person: the Manager. More than anyone else, the boss creates the conditions that directly determine people's ability to work well.

The Manager is the one who climbs the tallest tree, surveys the situation, and yells, "wrong jungle!"

Organizations are more in need of a vision and a compass and less in need of a road map. Organizations often don't know what the terrain ahead will be like or what will be needed to go through it. In these circumstances much depends on judgment at the time and an inner compass will always provide direction.

Effectiveness often depends not on how much effort we expend climbing the ladder, but on whether or not the ladder we are climbing is leaning against the right wall. Proactive powerful management must monitor environmental change, particularly customer habits and motives, and provide the energy necessary to organize resources in the right direction.

No matter what Managers set out to do - whether it's strategizing or mobilizing teams - their success is based on how they do it. Even if they get everything else right, if managers fail in the task of creating an upbeat mental attitude, nothing they do will function as well as it could or should.

The reason a Manager's manner - not what he does, but also how he does it - matters lies in the design of the human brain where the emotional centers depend upon external sources. In other words, we rely on connections with others for our own emotional stability. Research in intensive care units has exhibited that the soothing presence of another person not only lowers the patient's blood pressure but also slows the secretion of fats that block arteries. Whereas three or more incidents of severe stress within a year triple the death rate in socially detached middle-aged men they have no impact on the death rate of men who cultivate close relationships.

However, it is the manager who contributes the most to the emotional climate because everyone watches the boss. Employees take their emotional cues from the top. Even when the CEO works behind closed doors on another floor. His attitude affects the dispositions of his direct reports, and a domino effect ripples throughout the corporation's emotional climate. Careful observations of working groups in action revealed numerous ways the manager plays such a pivotal role in determining the shared emotions. Managers typically spoke more than anyone else, and what they said was listened to more carefully. Managers were usually the first to speak out on a subject, and when others made comments, their remarks were often referred to what the manager had said than to anyone else's comments. Because the manager's way of seeing things has special weight, managers manage meaning for a group, offering a way to interpret, and so react emotionally to a given situation.

But this impact goes beyond what a manager says. Even when managers are not talking, they are watched more carefully than anyone else in the group. Indeed, group members generally see the manager's emotional reaction as the most valid response, and so model their own on it - particularly in an ambiguous situation, where various members react differently. In a way, the manager sets the emotional standard.

Managers praise or criticize, offer support or turn a blind eye to an employee's needs. They can frame the team's mission in ways that give meaning to each employee's contribution – or not. They can guide in ways that give employees a sense of clarity and direction in their work.

How easily we catch a managers' emotional states, then, has to do with how expressively their faces, voices and gestures convey their feelings. The greater a manager's skill at transmitting emotions, the more forcefully the emotions will spread. Managers with that kind of talent are emotional magnets; people naturally gravitate to them. If one thinks about the leaders with whom people most want to work in an organization, they probably have this ability to exude upbeat feelings. It is one reason emotionally skilled managers attract talented people - for the privilege of working in their presence. Conversely, managers who emit the negative register - who are irritable, domineering, cold - repel people. Research has exhibited it: Optimistic, enthusiastic managers more easily retain their employees, compared with managers who tend toward negative moods.

Although emotions and feelings may seem trivial from a hardcore business point of view, they have real consequences for getting work done. A manager's mild anxiety can act as a signal that something needs more attention and profound thought. However, while mild anxiety can focus energy, prolonged distress can sabotage a manager's relationships and also hamper work performance by diminishing the brain's ability to process and interpret a situation. A good laugh, on the other hand, enhances the neural abilities crucial for good performance.

On the other hand a sour relationship with a boss can leave a person captive of that distress, with a mind preoccupied and a body unable to calm it's self. As a result, we naturally prefer being with people who are emotionally positive, in part because they make us feel good.

People who are upset have trouble reading emotions accurately in other people - decreasing the most basic skill needed for empathy, impairing their social skills. The percentage of time employees feel positive emotions at work turns out to be one of the strongest predictors of contentment, and therefore, for example, of how likely employees are to quit.

When employees feel good, they work at their best. Feeling good lubricates mental effectiveness, making employees better at understanding information and more flexible in their thinking. Upbeat moods, research suggests, make people view others in a more positive light. That in turn helps employees feel more optimistic about their ability to achieve a goal, enhances creativity and decision making skills, and predisposes them to be helpful. Moreover, research on humor at work suggests that playful laughter or a humorous anecdote can stimulate creativity, open lines of communication and trust, and, of course, make work more fun. Playful joking increases the likelihood of financial concessions during a negotiation.

Good moods prove especially significant when it comes to teams: The ability of a manager to lead a group into an enthusiastic, cooperative mood can determine its success. On the other hand, whenever emotional conflicts in a group suck energy from their shared challenges, a team's performance will suffer.

When we consider the results of a study of sixty-two CEOs and their top management teams we find significant data. The CEOs and their management team were assessed on how positive - energetic, enthusiastic, determined - they were. They were also asked how much conflict and clamor the top team experienced, that is, personality clashes, friction and emotional conflicts.

The study found that the more positive the overall moods of people in the top management team, the more co-operatively they worked together - and the better the company's results. There is a logarithm that predicts that relationship: For every 1 percent improvement in the service climate, there's a 2 percent increase in revenue.

Climate in itself does not establish performance. The factors deciding which organizations prove most fit in any given quarter are quite complex but analysis suggests that how people feel about working at a company- can account for up to 30 percent of business performance. Creating a positive environment and employee state of mind pays off in solid results.

If environment drives business results, what drives environment? Up to 70 percent of how employees perceive their organization's climate can be traced to the actions of one person: the manager. More than anyone else, the boss creates the settings that directly determine employees' ability to work well.

Creating Environment of Self Confidence

One of the manager's most important jobs is to maintain a positive, self-confident tone during ups and downs. Especially the downs when everyone else is feeling low, much like the circumstances around us these days, The manager maintains a positive attitude and absorbs the anxiety he feels.

Working with good managers fosters greater self-confidence in all constituents. Managers take actions and create conditions that strengthen their constituents' self-esteem and internal sense of effectiveness. From this process comes the repeated sentiment "my manager believes in me and so I can believe in myself."

In an innovative series of experiments, Stanford University professor Albert Bandura and University of Western Australia professor Robert Wood documented that self-confidence affects people's performance. In one study, managers were told that decision making was a skill developed through practice: the more one worked at it, the more capable one became. Other managers were told that decision making reflected their basic intellectual aptitude: the higher the underlying cognitive capacities, the better their decision making abilities. Working with a simulated organization, both groups of managers dealt with a series of production orders that required various staffing decisions and establishing different performance targets. Managers who believed that decision making was a skill that could be acquired set challenging goals for themselves, even in the face of difficult performance standards; used good problem-solving strategies; and encouraged organizational productivity. Their counterparts, who didn't believe they had necessary decision-making ability, lost confidence in themselves as they encountered difficulties. They lowered their aspirations for the organization, their problem solving skills deteriorated and organizational productivity declined.

Another interesting finding was that the managers

who lost confidence in their own judgment tended to find fault with their people. Indeed they were quite uncharitable about their employees, regarding them as incapable of being motivated and unworthy of supervisory effort: given the option, the managers would have fired many of their employees.

In another study, one group of managers was told that organizations and people are easily changeable or predictable. Another group was told, "work habits of employees are not that easily changeable, even by good guidance. Small changes do not necessarily improve overall outcomes." Those managers with the confidence that they could influence organizational outcomes by their actions maintained a higher level of performance than those who felt they could do little to change things. Those in the latter group lost faith in their capabilities. As their aspirations declined so did organizational performance levels.

As these studies illustrate, having confidence and believing in our ability to handle the job, no matter how difficult, are essential in promoting and sustaining consistent efforts. By communicating the belief that constituents can be successful, good managers help people extend themselves.

Although the effort may begin with some words of encouragement and support the most effective means of increasing people's self-confidence is achieved through actual experience; that is, providing them with an opportunity to perform successfully. An initial experience with success followed by a series of small successes over a period of time form the basis of an individual's self-confidence. The leader's challenge is to create situations for small wins, with each success building up the person's sense of competence. They invest in educating individuals to build their confidence and research has confirmed the effectiveness of this strategy. In Toronto, MICA Management Resources Corporation's survey of senior executives revealed that organizations that invested more than the average amount of money on training enjoyed higher levels of employee involvement and commitment, better levels of customer service, and greater understanding of and alignment with company vision and values. This finding was consistent with a recent Conference Board of Canada study showing that spending money on training and development was a profitable investment. These results should not come as any surprise, but apparently many companies and their managers have failed to realize that learning on the job is critical. In fact, over the past seventy years, it has contributed more to productivity increases than technology or capital.

Good managers don't overreact to human weaknesses. They don't feel built up when they discover the weaknesses of others. They are aware of weakness. But they realize that behavior and potential are two different things. They believe in the unseen potential of all people. They refuse to label other people, to stereotype and prejudge.

The truth is that one of the main reasons that winners win is that they think they can win. The possibility of achieving a desirable goal is the very ingredient that generates the energy necessary to achieve that goal and to tackle new ones. Therefore, one of the most valuable things that good managers do is build the determination and self-confidence in others.

Winners always throw themselves wholeheartedly into everything they do. Good enough is never good enough for them. They care deeply about their work. They believe that it has value and is important, and they approach it with a determination that just isn't found in people who are motivated by career aspirations alone. Good managers see everything in life as an opportunity to improve and grow. As a result, they work longer and harder than most people can even imagine.

Creating Harmony

Good managers align organizational structure, systems, and operational processes so that everyone contributes to achieving the mission and vision of meeting the needs of customers and other stakeholders. They don't interfere with it, they don't compete with it, and they don't dominate it. They're there for one purpose - to contribute to it. Far and away the greatest leverage of the principle of harmony comes when people are in alignment with the mission, vision and strategy. When people are filled with true understanding of the needs, when they share a powerful commitment to accomplishing the vision, when they are invited to create and continually improve the structure and systems that will meet the needs, then there is harmony. Without these human conditions, there cannot be world-class quality. Good managers improve and harmonize almost any situation they get into.

In team endeavors they build on their strengths and strive to compliment their weaknesses with the strengths of others. Delegation for results is easy and natural to them, since they believe in others' strengths and capacities. And since they are not threatened by the fact that others are better in some ways, they feel no need to supervise them closely.

When good managers negotiate and communicate with others in seemingly adversarial situations, they learn to separate the people from the problem. They focus on the other person's interests and concerns rather than fight over positions. Gradually others discover their sincerity and become part of a creative problem-solving process. Together they arrive at synergistic solutions, which are usually much better than any of the original proposals, as opposed to compromise solutions wherein both parties give and take a little.

Under the guidance of an emotionally sensitive manager, people make decisions collaboratively and feel secure enough to accept input from others. It is not my way or your way but a better way. Good managers form an emotional bond that helps constituents stay focused even amid profound change and uncertainty. Perhaps most important, connecting with others at an emotional level makes work more meaningful. We all know what it feels like to share in the excitement of a moment, the elation of completing a job well done. These feelings drive people to do things together that no individual could or would do. And it is the emotionally sensitive manager who knows how to bring about that kind of bonding.

On the other hand, if a manager lacks this emotional connection with the employees, people may be going through the motions of their work but doing merely a mediocre job rather than giving their best. Without a healthy dose of heart, a supposed manager may manage - but he does not lead.

Good managers high in self-awareness are attuned to their own inner signals, recognizing how their feelings affect them and their job performance. They are attuned to their guiding values and can often intuit the best course of action, seeing the big picture in a complex situation. Emotionally self-aware managers can be candid and authentic, able to speak openly about their emotions or with conviction about their guiding vision.

Good managers understand deeply the hurts and bruises, joys and struggles, aims and aspirations of their constituents. Through carefully listening and being sensitive to the needs of others, they can recognize their needs and offer ways to fill them. However, people will follow the advice and recommendations only when they trust the manager's competence and believe that they have their best interest at heart.

Understanding and appreciating constituents' needs and values – and thus establishing credibility – is made more difficult in today's complex environment. Corporations are of necessity becoming more global, employing much more diverse work forces, responding to more demanding customers with wide-ranging needs, and facing more concerned shareholders. They are also developing closer relationships with fewer suppliers and are being asked to pay more attention to the needs of the communities in which they exist. This requires effort and skill but one benefit is that a natural byproduct of attending to other people is that they in turn come to trust the manager and the manager to trust them.

Harvard Business School professor John Kotter provides support for the perspective that organizations with adaptive, performance enhancing cultures have outperformed non-adaptive, unhealthy ones precisely because of their emphasis on attending to all of their constituencies (that is, customers, stockholders, and employees). By contrast, they found that in organizations with non-adaptive and unhealthy cultures "most managers mainly care about themselves, their immediate work group, or some product (or technology) associated with that work group."

With increasing clarity, executives are beginning to understand the need to balance high tech with high touch. They are seeing the necessity of more cooperation and a greater focus on others. Scholars and executives alike have recognized the impact of corporate culture and the ways that shared values make a difference. As facilitators and coaches, today's managers place greater emphasis on understanding the concerns of their work group members and supporting the efforts of others than did their counterparts just a decade or so ago and hence focus more on building greater harmony.

Creating Energy and Enthusiasm

All organizations inherently have energy because they are made up of people, and people have energy. But in successful organizations, people seem to have more energy, and they certainly use it more productively. While the losers waste their energy on negative activities such as internal politics and resisting change demanded by the marketplace, the winners use theirs positively to overcome problems and meet new challenges. They do this because their top managers understand that positive energy produces positive results. They use energy like ideas and values as a competitive tool. And they consciously work at creating positive energy in everyone else in the organization.

Ideas and values are strong motivators however ideas and values alone cannot carry the day. Winning organizations do their jobs better than others. And in a highly competitive world, this means that they work faster and with greater energy. Therefore, good managers not only encourage people to have good ideas and develop strong values, but they also take deliberate actions to generate energy and to channel it to productive uses.

Good managers design their management processes so that fresh ideas bubble to the surface and people are energized. They do this by ensuring that people feel that the process is worthwhile, that conclusive decisions are reached and that those decisions do, in fact, get carried out. To do this, managers create operating mechanisms through which they assure that people are adequately prepared to make decisions. And most decisions that are made are substantive and that there is systematic follow-up to make sure the decision is implemented.

The countenance of good managers is cheerful, pleasant, and happy. Their attitude is optimistic, positive and upbeat. Their spirit is enthusiastic and hopeful. This positive energy is like an energy field or an aura that surrounds them and that similarly charges or changes weaker, negative energy fields around them. They also attract and magnify smaller positive energy fields. When they come into contact with strong, negative energy sources, they tend either to neutralize or to sidestep this negative energy. Sometimes they will simply leave it, walking away from its poisonous orbit. Wisdom gives them a sense of how strong it is and a sense of humor and timing in dealing with it.

Be aware of the effect of your own energy and understand how you radiate and direct it. And in the middle of confusion or contention or negative energy, strive to be a peacemaker, a harmonizer, to undo or reverse destructive energy.

The enormous physical energy of these managers excites and energizes everyone around them. They set a pace that brings others up to speed. Still, as impressive as their physical energy is, it is their emotional energy, and their ability to evoke emotional energy in others, that truly marks them as a breed apart. How they display it isn't as important as the simple fact that they are supremely engaged by their work, and it shows. A winning leader can turn even the most mundane of meetings into an exciting encounter.

Highly competitive people are often loners, but in good managers, it is their very competitiveness that drives them to work so hard at energizing and coaching other people. This is because they are determined that their organizations succeed, and they know that they can't do everything themselves. They understand strategically that they need everyone in the organization giving his or her best efforts. So they work very hard to make that happen.

Good managers instinctively realize that every meeting and every activity has the potential to create or destroy emotional energy. So they deliberately develop an operating style and design management processes with an eye to their effect on people's energy levels.

One sign of a good manager is a group of followers who echo the manager's enthusiastic energy. Enthusiasm is an integral part of a positive work environment. On an emotional level enthusiasm is as pivotal as any other positive emotion. The glue that holds people together in a team, and that commits people to an organization, is the emotions they feel. So if the emotion holding the people together in the organization is enthusiasm even better. The significance of enthusiasm is such that the Latin term that the word 'enthusiasm' comes from means 'god within'.

Occasional team celebrations and motivational events provide energy spurts but they don't have staying power. Energy that carries a team the farthest is created when members know they are a part of something special and feel good about themselves and one another. Energy boosters include focusing on what makes the team special, helping people to use their potential talents, ensuring that members feel good about themselves, having fun together and creating a team environment in which members know they can count on one another.

Energy Siphons

Working against the cumulative positive energy there are also energy siphons that weaken the team by constantly draining energy. The strongest siphons are negative environments. In some companies small issues are regularly escalated into major problems; in others, the first thing people do when something goes wrong is look for someone, other than themselves, to blame. Ensuring the boosters are at work in your team and the siphons are not is not difficult but it takes vigilance. You have to decide that keeping the energy level of your team high is a priority.

In some environments, members become addicted to sensationalism and negativity. Take a small incident, add emotion and circulate it throughout the team and you'll end up with something much larger than the issue deserved. These teams are emotional escalators that unintentionally carry situations over the top. They are often led by individuals whose nature is to react quickly and emotionally rather than to respond thoughtfully. The manager usually works closely with the team members and shares openly with them. This strength becomes a negative when the manager also shares his emotional reactions to issues. The teams under such a manager are constantly dealing with self-created crisis. Their mountain building wastes valuable energy and distracts them from the job at hand. In addition, this culture is an assumption generator and each assumption is capable of creating ongoing problems.

The ability to step back from a situation, examine it dispassionately and respond thoughtfully is a key leadership success factor. Emotional responses siphon energy from you and your team that you can't afford to waste.

Creating a Culture of Hope and Optimism

Most experts expect the stressful economic, social, and political upheavals to persist for many years and in some cases even get worse. Given these gloomy economic and political forecasts, organizations are in great need of hopeful and resilient constituents. The only antidote to the increased cynicism and stresses of our time is renewed faith in human capacity and an intensely optimistic belief that together we can overcome the difficulties of today and tomorrow. "Keep hope alive" is the manager's battle cry.

In keeping hope alive, good managers demonstrate their faith and confidence by first accepting responsibility for the quality of their lives and for those of their constituents. Even when everything goes wrong or when resounding challenges occur good managers bounce back by taking charge of the situation.

When managers act in ways that uplift our spirits

and restore our belief in the future, they strengthen their own personal credibility. Constituents look for managers who demonstrate an enthusiastic and genuine belief in the capacity of others, who strengthen people's will, who supply the means to achieve, and who express optimism for the future. Constituents want managers who remain passionate despite obstacles and setbacks. In today's uncertain times, leaders with a positive, confident, can-do approach to life and business are desperately needed.

Managers must keep hope alive. They must strengthen our belief that life's struggle will produce a more promising tomorrow. Such faith results from an intimate and supportive relationship, one based on mutual participation in the process of renewal.

Good managers sustain hope by painting positive images of the future. They arouse optimistic feelings and enable their constituents to hold positive thoughts about the possibilities of success and in challenging times struggle alongside others. They do not hide from suffering.

Good managers drop by for a visit to see how people are doing. They offer a shoulder to lean on and give advice and counsel. They may even devise a special training apparatus. And good managers keep hope alive when they recognize the dedication of others to pursue excellence, especially when the struggle is a challenge.

Because of their expectation that things will work out for the best, optimists look at the future and see attractive possibilities. These motivate optimists to be proactive and to take actions that improve their work performance and their physical and mental health. In contrast, pessimists envision negative scenarios and see probabilities of failure.

The habitual ways that optimists and pessimists

explain why events happen differ dramatically. Martin Seligman found that pessimists see failed events as permanent and personal defeats. They blamed themselves for the bad things that happen and they ascribe the good things to conditions not under their control. Optimists, by contrast, tend to see defeats as temporary and having specific causes. They blame circumstances for the bad things that happen. And when good outcomes occur, optimists believe that these things always happen to them, that positive events enhance everything they do, and that good things come from their actions and not the circumstances.

Optimism is essential to strengthening credibility. Managers with their eyes on an ideal and strong image of tomorrow reflect optimistic outlooks. In expressing their convictions that it will work out for the best and be better than the past, optimists instill confidence in others. Constituents begin to adopt a similar attitude. When they look to the future, they also see the possibilities of success.

Based on Seligman's research, managers who want to inspire optimism would employ a number of distinct strategies. When a failure or setback occurs, they do not blame themselves or the people working on the project. Instead, they find situational circumstances that contributed to the failure and convey a belief that the situation is likely to be temporary, not permanent. They stress that the failure or setback means a problem only in this one instance and not in everything. When success occurs and milestones are reached, managers who want to breed optimism attribute success to the individuals in the group. They convey a belief that many more victories are at hand and predict that good fortune will be with them for a long time.

None of this is to suggest that managers should avoid getting people to accept personal responsibility. Optimism and personal responsibility are not mutually exclusive. People can either accept responsibility for a problem and its consequences with an optimistic attitude that will enable them to persist in solving it, or can view it with a pessimistic attitude that defeats them before they start. Which person would you rather have on your team? Which manager would you rather be?

Seligman advises, "At the head of the corporation must be a CEO, sage enough and flexible enough to balance the optimistic vision of the planners against the negativity of the bureaucrats. Good managers are hopeful about the future – and yielding enough to heed words of caution. Seligman refers to such people as flexible optimists.

Optimism, like hope, does not mean simply waiting for good things to happen; it means acting in ways that create positive futures. But such futures do not always come easily. Sometimes, if not always, struggles and suffering are necessary to achieve greatness. As in athletics, success in business is governed by the rule of "no pain, no gain." Even the hardiest of world-class competitors pull muscles, strain ligaments, tear tendons, and break bones. No one – athlete, business leader, or government leader – ever hopes for injury, but each experience it. And each has to work through the pain. Managers who are not willing to suffer personally the pain and strain of high-level competition will find that his credibility quickly diminishes.

For good managers suffering breeds increased passion for the goal or cause. The myth is that passion comes from joy. It does not. The word passion has its roots in the Greek and Latin words for suffering. The most passionate people are those who suffered the most. They have risked their independence, their fortunes, their health, and sometimes their lives for people and a purpose beyond themselves. Passion earned from suffering is inspiring.

Creating a Culture of Courage and Perseverance

A fierce determination to succeed is the characteristic of those who survive and thrive in all arenas. Look, for example, at the late Sam Walton, founder of Wal-Mart, the world's largest retailer. Determination, drive, and resilience were evident in Walton at the time he opened his very first retail operation, a little Ben Franklin franchise store in Newport, Arkansas. Walton wanted to build it into the best store in town and he did. It was so successful in fact that his landlord wanted it for himself and his son. The landlord put the squeeze on Walton and did not renew the lease, knowing Walton had no other place to go in the small town. Instead, he offered to buy the franchise. Walton had no choice in that instance but to give up the store and move on.

"It was," Walton says, "the low point in my business life… It really was like a nightmare. I had built the best variety store in the whole region and worked hard in the community – done everything right – and now I was being kicked out of town."

But Walton was not down for long. "It's not just a corny saying that you can make a positive out of most negatives if you work at it hard enough. I've always thought of problems as challenges, and this one wasn't any different… I had to pick myself and get on with it, do it all over again, only even better this time." As much as his retailing savvy, that attitude – making positives out of negatives, thinking of problems as challenges, working hard, doing even better – enabled Walton to succeed.

Anita Roddick's is another retailing success story. Roddick is managing director of the highly successful, London-based Body Shop International. She started the business on her own in 1976 with one store; then with her partner and husband, Gordon, she enlarged the business to more than eight hundred stores today. In England, Roddick has been named Businesswoman of the Year, Communicator of the Year, and Retailer of the Year and has received the Queen's Award for Export and the United Nations Environmentalist Award for her support in protecting and restoring the natural world. She is clearly a success; Inc. magazine has even said that she has changed business forever.

Roddick's intensity fuels her and infects all around her. She says, "To me the desire to create and to have control over your own life, irrespective of the politics of the time or the social structures, was very much part of the human spirit. What I did not fully realize was that work could open the doors to my heart." With the doors of her heart open, she has created a market for her natural body care products, expanded her business globally, and demonstrated that a business can be successful serving customers, associates, shareholders, and communities while also preserving the environment and contributing to world peace.

But for all her success, Roddick has had her share of setbacks. In the beginning she and her husband ran a small hotel and a restaurant. Writing about why their Littlehampton restaurant, Paddington's, didn't work out, Roddick explains, "The reason was quite simple – we had done everything wrong. It was the wrong kind of establishment in the wrong street in the wrong town, launched at the wrong time. We were young, we thought we knew it all and we had certainly not bothered to take any advice. We thought we could impose our will on our customers and sell gourmet food in an egg-and-chips town." But the Roddicks were not down for long: "What saved us was our willingness to recognize that we were wrong and our ability to move swiftly on to the next idea."

Good managers acknowledge reality but do not dwell on the threat. Instead, they see change as an opportunity for renaissance and learning; they move quickly to mobilize personal and group resources. They believe they can influence the outcome and can turn the tide of events to their advantage. They do not become bitter or alienated; instead, they become engaged and committed. They do not dissolve into despair but resolve to act quickly and zestfully.

Good managers are proactive. They do not wait to be told what to do. They believe that it is possible to exert internal control, rather than being controlled externally by others or events. They recognize that they cannot control all of what goes on in life, but they are determined to be in charge of the quality of their own lives. Maybe the company has no overarching vision or plan; for good managers, even this barrier is not an insurmountable roadblock. They search for their chances to make something happen; they also instill this attitude in constituents, creating ways that they can take charge of at least their own responsibilities.

Managers who are truly inspirational, who demonstrate courage and passion, are the first to suffer. They are the first to step out into the unknown, to confront self-doubt, to suffer defeat and disappointment, and return to triumph. A manager who risks embarrassment and ruin and yet succeeds in maintaining the strength of conviction gives others courage. We are uplifted by those who show us that we will survive. Someone who sits by in comfort while ordering others to suffer only stands to lose respect.

When managers share in the pain they develop compassion for others who are suffering. Compassion means "to suffer together". Only those who have suffered with their constituents can genuinely uplift others. Only those who felt the pain of loss and yearning for fulfillment can truly inspire. It may be that one of the reasons for increased cynicism over the last several years is the perception that those in leadership positions have not suffered along with their constituents that they are unwilling to risk what they have gained for the sake of the cause that they care only for themselves. It is ironic that those in power most risk losing everything when they are least willing to give up just a little.

Scholars, including Abraham Zaleznik, Eric Ericson, Jon Gardner and James MacGregor Burns, all have written about the importance of early childhood experiences and hardships in shaping character. Having suffered and recovered gives people a self-confidence and self-reliance that allows them to be unencumbered by the need to bend to popular will. It is this freedom that gives them the ability to make decisions based on reality, even though they may be unpopular or contrary to conventional wisdom.

Most people acknowledge that perseverance is important but the definition of trying hard is very personal. Do you try 2 or 3 or 50 times? Do you work on something for an hour, a day or a month? It depends on where one sits on the Stick to It scale. Those who sit at the high end of the scale and have tenacious lock on their goal can achieve remarkable things.

An exceptional example of persistence personified is Starbucks' founder Howard Schultz. He was turned down by 217 of the 242 investors he talked to when raising venture capital in Starbuck' early days. How many rejections would be required before most of us would shrug our shoulders and decide that it mustn't have been such a good idea after all.

Are there times when it's appropriate to throw in the towel and recognize that a goal was poorly chosen and is not achievable? Of course there are – once every effort has been made. But when the goal is compelling and the desire is great, 'every' is defined very differently than it otherwise might be.

Ultimately, your perseverance will be a major contributor to your success. Winston Churchill used to say "It's not good enough to say we are doing our best. We must do what has to be done."

Creating a Culture of Success

A culture of success is felt more than seen. A positive energy and confidence can be felt within the group. You also hear it. If team members are located on-site together, you will hear frequent laughter and a buzz of quiet conversation that is quite different from idle chit chat. There is a sense of pro-activity and urgency. Members embrace tasks and run with them. Small wins are celebrated and members look for opportunities to celebrate their teammates' achievements. A feeling of anticipation is obvious, as though something exciting is just around the corner. You can also recognize cultures of success by what is missing. Negativity and gossip are noticeably absent.

Some basic actions and attitudes nurture either success or failure in any organization.

How to best feed a culture of success? First check your own language and demeanor. Do you present yourself like a winner? Do you carry an aura of success into the team? Your energy, confidence and positive attitude are catching, as is any hint of negativity or defeat.

Defensive comments such as "We're never going to make it" that reflect discouragement or "We can't help it if we don't have the resources we need" are sure to give failure a quick growth spurt, as are ominous comments such as "If we don't make it this time…." Even the more subtle sighing, head shaking and lack of enthusiasm feed failure. Not celebrating the small successes and not recognizing individual performance also feed failure.

Mediocrity is fed by being satisfied if we can repeat and perhaps improve just slightly on what we accomplished yesterday. Too often a "fair showing" is all that is expected. A culture of mediocrity thrives when people are satisfied with being reasonably successful. People often label this attitude as "being realistic." "We can only expect so much from people," they say. "You can't win all the time."

A culture of mediocrity is a greater threat than one of failure. Behaviors such as negativity that favor failure are usually obvious enough to be noticed and eliminated if the effort is made. But mediocrity can live on without dramatically drawing attention to its self. For example, managers attempting to be sensitive to pressures staff may be facing often inadvertently encourage mediocrity. In cultures of mediocrity, deadlines are allowed to slip too often, performance that is less than stellar is accepted and people manage to "get out of" important meetings.

Being obsessed with the key requirements for success prevents the team from being caught up in activities that do not directly contribute to results.

Having a strong and clear focus provides another great advantage that is not fully appreciated by many managers. A clear focus allows team members increased self-direction. If members know absolutely what success for the team looks like and what must take priority in order to realize that picture, they will be better equipped to make highly effective tactical decisions on their own. You can then achieve better results faster, with the additional advantage that members will have a sense of ownership – one of the ingredients of a culture of success.

Creating Uniqueness

Creating Uniqueness anywhere is about differentiation – what makes a company, department or team different from others that perform a similar service or sell a similar product? The key is not to just be seen as unique externally but to be seen as unique first by employees. The kind of uniqueness that creates the sense of pride that sustains it includes two components. First, the group's uniqueness is not defined only by the fact that it does things differently but also by the fact that there is a worthwhile purpose in what it is doing. This leads to the second component: the group's unique purpose has an emotional appeal to the head. A unique purpose appeals to the heart. People want to be associated with something meaningful.

If there is nothing to differentiate you, you won't have

the fuel to have the competitive edge. No competitive edge means a very short lifeline. Any team that aims to be above the ordinary must have practices that are unique and that members are proud of. The more unique and successful the practices and the more they are played up, the greater the team spirit. Practices that might be considered ordinary, such as excellent customer service, become unique if embraced with a passion.

Uniqueness doesn't have to pre-exist in the nature of a product or service. In fact, it seldom does. It's up to the manager and the team to create uniqueness. It means doing something so differently or so extraordinarily well that you stand out. Clients and your partners, both internal and external, can't help noticing. But it goes even further than that. There is a conscious decision to be different. The uniqueness is captured not only in the team's practices but in its destination and in how the team describes where it is going and how it will get there.

Creating Leaders

Besides instilling confidence in people around them good managers encourage leadership qualities in others. They are aware that leadership is a set of skills and practices that can be learned regardless of whether or not one is in a formal management position. They know that leadership is not conferred by title or degree. Their ideal goal is that united in a common cause, every member of the team becomes responsible for providing leadership. They know that self-led teams outperform teams that are tightly managed by controlling supervisors.

Good managers turn their constituents into leaders.

This is the essence of how good managers get extraordinary things done in their organizations: they enable people to act. It is not a case of the manager doing something or even telling others what to do but of everyone wanting to work together for a common purpose, one that is aligned with shared values.

Empowerment is an important concept but one often misunderstood. The problem with empowerment is that it suggests that this is something managers magically give or do for others. But people already have tremendous power. It is a matter of expanding their opportunities to use themselves in service of a common and meaningful purpose. What is often called empowerment is really just taking off the chains and letting people loose. Managers in this sense are liberators.

Good managers manage to empower the constituents without losing control. First, specify desired results. Discuss what results you expect. Be specific about the quantity and quality. Set budget and schedule. Commit people to getting the results, but then let them determine the best methods and means. Set target dates or timelines for the accomplishment of your objectives. These objectives essentially represent the overlap between the organizational strategy, goals, and job design, and the personal values, goals, needs, and capabilities. The concept of a mutually gratifying solution suggests that the managers and employees clarify expectations and mutually commit themselves to getting desired results.

Second, set some guidelines. Communicate whatever principles, policies and procedures are considered essential to getting desired results. Mention as few procedures as possible to give as much freedom as possible. Organizational policy and procedure manuals should be brief, focusing primarily on the principles behind the policy and procedures. Then, as the circumstances change, people are not frozen - they can still function, using their own initiative and good judgment and doing what's necessary to get the desired results within the value framework of the company.

Guidelines should also identify no - no's or failure paths that experience has identified as inimical to accomplishing organizational goals or maintaining organizational values. Many a management-by-objectives MBO program goes down in flames because these no - no's are not clearly identified. People are given this feeling that they have almost unlimited flexibility and freedom to do whatever is necessary to accomplish agreed - upon results and end up re-inventing the wheel, encountering certain organizational sacred cows, upsetting apple carts, getting blown out of the saddle, and becoming increasingly gun shy about ever exercising initiative again.

The general attitude then becomes, "Let's forget about this MBO stuff. Just tell us what you want us to do." Their expectations are blasted, and the scar tissue on their behinds is so thick that they begin to see the job purely as a means to an economic end and seek to satisfy their higher needs elsewhere. No leaders are created.

Management must empower its people in the deepest sense and remove the barriers and obstacles it has created that crush and defeat the inherent commitment, creativity, and quality service that people are otherwise prepared to offer. To receive joy and pride in one's work is the right of all. And it is the management practices that prevent it!

Another way good managers create leaders is by giving them choices. Choice builds commitment. Choice necessitates ownership. Jack Stack, CEO, explains what ownership means for his constituents at Springfield Remanufacturing Corporation: "We have a company filled with people who not only are owners, but who think and act like owners rather than employees. That's an important distinction. Getting people to think and act like owners went far beyond giving them equity.... Owners, real owners, don't have to be told what to do – they can figure it out for themselves. They have all the knowledge, understanding and information they need to make a decision, and they have the motivation and the will to act fast. "Ownership is not a set of legal rights. It's a state of mind." Good managers create real owners by making certain people have choices to make about what they do, especially in how shared values are implemented.

People have enormous talent, ingenuity, intelligence, and creativity. Most of it lies dormant. When you have true alignment toward a common vision, a common mission, you begin to co-mission with those people. Individual purpose and mission are commingled with the mission of the organization. When these purposes overlap, great synergy is created. A fire is ignited within people and it unleashes their latent talent, ingenuity and creativity to do whatever is necessary or consistent with the principles agreed upon to accomplish their common values, vision, and mission in serving customers and other stakeholders.

Questions to Ask

1) Do your employees enjoy what they do?

2) Are most of your employees visionary and inspiring or cooperative and trustworthy?

3) Do you maintain a positive self confident tone during ups and downs?

4) Do you make your constituents feel like winners?

5) Do you instill leadership qualities in others and empower them?

6) Do you give people choices?

7) Do you design management processes so that fresh ideas pop up?

8) Do you have a fierce determination to succeed?

9) Can you create uniqueness in an ordinary product?

10) Do you accept responsibility for the quality of your life and the life of your constituents?

Motivation

Two things are not a source of true motivation in the long run; financial inducement and the fear of getting fired. People who work for a paycheck and not because they like what they do work as hard as they have to in order to get paid. In a survey of the work force done a few years ago employees put factors like working with people who treat them with respect, and a challenging and interesting job description, and recognition for good work, and a chance to develop skills, and job security, and working for efficient managers were all ranked by employees ahead of a higher pay as motivating factors. Fear is just as poor a motivator. Companies that are run on the basis of fear will end up with a work force of resentful employees, just itching to take advantage of the organizational system.

There is only one way to get anybody to do anything and that is by making that person want to do it. There is no other way. Of course, you can make someone want to give you his wallet by sticking a knife in his ribs. You can make your employees cooperate by threatening to fire them until your back is turned. You can make a child do what you want by spanking. But these crude methods have sharply undesirable consequences. They serve to do exactly the opposite of what you are trying to achieve, i.e. motivate.

There is no single incentive that motivates all of your people all of the time. Also different people are motivated by different thing at different times. But the biggest mistake that leaders make is misunderstanding what motivates most of their followers most of the time.

We're constantly irrational about ourselves. And that has profound impact on organizations. Unfortunately, most organizations take a negative view of their people. They verbally chastise participants for sub-par performance. They call for risk taking but punish even tiny failures. They want innovation but kill the spirit of the innovator. They design systems that seem calculated to tear down their workers' self image. They might not mean to be doing that, but they are.

They take care of the individual's physiological needs and believe that to be sufficient. Besides the physiological needs there is the need to feel 'important'. A great motivating factor is to give someone a sense of purpose, the feeling that he or she is working for a valuable, meaningful goal. That's where true motivation comes from - motivation not just to go through the motions of working, motivation to excel.

And the way to motivate people and to give them the motivation to excel is to recognize them. Include them. Encourage them. Train them. Ask for their opinions. Praise them. Let them make decisions. Share the glory with them. Seek their advice and follow it when you can. Make them understand how appreciated they are. Encourage them to take risks. Give them the freedom to work as they see fit, and convey your belief in their abilities by getting out of their way. The best way to put business first is to put people first.

Dwight Eisenhower said "You do not lead by hitting people over the head that is assault not leadership. I would persuade a man to go along because once he has been persuaded he will stick. If I scare him, he will stay just as long as he is scared, and then he is gone."

Get people interested in what they do. Dramatize it. Communicate its significance in the grand scheme of things. Give them ownership.

Once this basic principle is recognized and understood, it's really quite easy to dream up all kinds of specific motivational techniques. But three important concepts of human behavior underlie them all.

Employees must be included in all parts of the process, every step of the way. They should know how their work contributes to the ultimate vision of the organization. Teamwork is the key here, not hierarchy.

Appreciate that no one thing would motivate all the people all of the time. People must be treated as individuals. Sometimes incentives have to be employee specific. Always acknowledge the importance of people and show them respect. They are people first, employees second. However you do it, have it done. Let the people in your life know that you respect them, that you appreciate their work, that they are important to you and that you want them to learn, grow and reach their potential.

Superior work must be recognized, encouraged and rewarded. Never forget to notice it. Everyone responds to expectations. If you treat people as if they are capable and smart -and get out of the way- that's exactly how they will perform. Acknowledge a job well done. Don't be the disapproving parent many of us grew up with. Those were the parents who didn't congratulate their kids for getting A on the Report Card. They just expected it. Remember how disappointing that was? Well, it's still disappointing. There's still a little child in every one of us, waiting to be praised. So don't forget: People want to be told when they've done a good job. Use praise liberally and often.

Another scientist by the name of Frederick Herzberg built on Maslow's work and collected data on job attitude among employees in hundreds of companies. From studying these data, he concluded that people have two categories of needs that affect satisfaction or dissatisfaction with a job.

The first category he called hygiene needs. He gave them this name because these needs serve the function of preventative medicine in the workplace. They prevent job dissatisfaction. They are also distinguished by the fact that these needs are never completely satisfied. You have to keep maintaining them, or you lose performance. You can't improve performance with them. But if your organization is already performing well, you can maintain these high standards with the hygiene factors. Hygiene factors include money, status, treatment and security.

According to Herzberg, motivators are satisfying factors that relate to the job itself. They involve feelings of achievement, recognition for accomplishment, challenging work, increased responsibility, growth, and development. These are the factors that produce job satisfaction as contrasted with the hygiene needs that only prevent job dissatisfaction.

Instilling Enthusiasm

Key to successful performance with workers is instilling enthusiasm a quality that organizations can earn but not compel.

What we normally call 'motivation' is the space between a desire to do something and genuine zeal. When we are enthusiastic, either the task is very rewarding in its own right or the external rewards are great enough to make it an attractive proposition. In business, when people are enthusiastic about their work, they create a business culture that is a pleasure to work in and it acts as a magnet to attract others. Customers like to deal with people who enjoy their work and companies prosper when everyone works from choice, with passion and energy. This kind of energy is priceless.

Unfortunately, you can create aversion and inertia much more easily than willingness and enthusiasm. It is easy. For a start, do not listen to what people want or what is important to them. Or, even worse, make a show of finding out what they want and then ignore it. When employees are asked about what sort of office they want, what sort of structure, how they want to work, they get excited and enthusiastic. When nothing happens or when something completely different is imposed, that is worse than not being asked at all.

Another good way to de-motivate people is to ignore their achievements and take good work for granted, but immediately comment on the slightest drop in standards. Act as if people are not trustworthy and ask them to account for all their time, question any time away from work.

Change, Please

Good managers tap the energy and passion that come from what matters to people. Leaders may also offer external rewards to make it worthwhile. In business, this brings us to the perennial key management question, debated in boardrooms ever since people came together: How do you get people to want to work?

Most people in management positions try to manage performance by telling other people what to do or not to do. They tell others to work harder, to show more initiative, and to be creative. They order, command, issue memos, circulate policy statements, conduct meetings, develop and circulate scorecards. In the technical jargon of performance management gurus this is called providing people with antecedents.

The problem with antecedents is that they don't work very well or for very long. People may change their behavior temporarily, but when they aren't being watched they just go back to their old ways.

To manage performance effectively another way to influence behavior has to be implemented. In addition to providing an antecedent to get behavior started something else has to be provided after the behavior occurs to increase or decrease the probability that it will be repeated. For example, in addition to asking people to get their work done on time they can be provided with a reward, recognition, or praise when they submit their reports on time, and they can be fined, fired, or otherwise punished when they are late. The technical jargon for what comes after the behavior is a consequence.

The message that comes through so poignantly is that we like to think of ourselves as winners. The lesson that good managers have to teach is that we must design systems that continually reinforce this notion; most people are made to feel that they are winners. Their people by and large make their targets and quotas, because the targets and quotas are set (often by the people themselves) to allow that to happen.

The good managers do not focus on producing a lot of winners but they make certain that once the winning occurs it is celebrated. Their systems make extraordinary use of non-monetary incentives. They are full of hoopla.

The Power of Positive Reinforcement

Positive reinforcement not only shapes behavior but also teaches and in the process enhances our own self-image. To give a negative example first, suppose that someone gets punished for "not treating a customer well." Not only does he not know what specifically to do in order to improve; he might well respond by "learning" to avoid customers altogether. "Customer" rather than "treating a customer badly," has become associated with punishment. On the other hand, if someone tells us via a compliment from a "mystery shopper" that we "just acted in the best traditions of ABC Corporation in responding to Mrs. Smith's minor complaint," well, that's quite different. What we are now likely to get is an employee out beating the bushes to find more Mrs. Smiths to treat well. He or she has learned that a specific behavior pattern leads to rewards and has at the same time satisfied the insatiable human need to enhance one's self-image.

Positive reinforcement has an intriguing property. It nudges good things onto agenda instead of ripping things off the agenda. Life in business, as otherwise, is fundamentally a matter of attention – how we spend our time. Thus management's most significant output is getting others to shift attention in desirable directions. There are only two ways to accomplish such a shift. First, we attempt through positive reinforcement to lead people gently over a period of time to pay attention to new activities. This is a subtle shaping process. Or we can simply try to wrestle undesirable traits off the agenda. Ripping items off an agenda leads to either overt or covert resistance: "I'll get out of the office, if you insist, but I'll spend the time in the local pub." The positively reinforced behavior slowly comes to occupy a larger and larger share of time and attention. By definition, something less desirable begins to drop off the agenda. But it drops off the agenda on the basis of our sorting process. The stuff that falls off is what we want to push off in order to make room for the positively reinforced items. The difference in approach is substantial. If, by force of time alone, we choose to push a low-priority item off, then it is highly unlikely that we will cheat on ourselves and try to do more of the less attractive behavior. So the use of positive reinforcement goes with the flow rather than against it.

As Skinner notes, the way the reinforcement is carried out is more important than the amount. First, it ought to be specific, incorporating as much information content as possible. Second, the reinforcement should have immediacy. Third, the system of feedback mechanisms should take account of achievability. Major events are not common, so the system should reward small wins. The fourth characteristic is that a fair amount of the feedback comes in the form of intangible but ever - so meaningful attention from top management. Finally, Skinner asserts that regular reinforcement loses impact because it comes to be expected. Thus unpredictable and intermittent reinforcements work better. Moreover, small rewards are frequently more effective than large ones. Big bonuses often become political, and they discourage legions of workers who don't get them but think they deserve them. Remember, we all think we are winners.

Motivating Rabbits and Donkeys

The problem with the 'carrot and stick' approach is that besides the fact that it treats people like rabbits and donkeys is that it does not work. Managers who try to substitute empathy with rewards are faced with a problem. Rewards and punishment both come from the outside, whereas motivation comes from the inside. Too great an emphasis on rewards and punishments gives the insidious message that the work itself is intrinsically hard and unsatisfying and people have to be tempted or threatened to do it at all.

The 'carrot' approach is the basis of incentives, bonuses and rewards. It works on the principle that people are motivated by rewards. Does it work? Yes. Rewards are good for overcoming apathy and inertia. Do they produce creative work? Not necessarily. People are not mechanical and predictable they change and adapt any system of rewards to their own ends. Also, what starts as an extra bonus soon gets taken for granted and becomes normal, just as we get accustomed to background music. We enjoy it then we expect it. But we notice when it stops! So rewards can de-motivate in the long term unless you keep cranking them up.

A reward is only a reward if it is valued by the recipient. Obvious perhaps, but all of us have seen many examples where management has offered incentives that no one wants. Money is one type of reward and tends to be overused. Everyone deserves a fair financial reward and good salaries should be paid, but paying money to try to get people to work faster or smarter does not usually work well.

Extraordinary Results from Ordinary People

So how can you force employees to do an extraordinary job? The truth is you cannot. People can never be forced to do an extraordinary job. They will perform extraordinarily only if they want to. The challenge is stimulating them with a reason to want to.

People will only want to perform extraordinarily if they feel like an important part of the organization. That's why employees need to be respected and included in a corporate vision they can embrace. That's why people need a stake in their work lives. That's why their successes need to be rewarded, praised, and celebrated. That's why their failures need to be handled gingerly.

Good management is patient, usually boring coalition building. It is the purposeful seeding of cabals that will hopefully result in the appropriate ferment in the bowels of the organization. It is meticulously shifting the attention of the institution through the mundane language of management systems. It is altering agendas so that new priorities get enough attention. It is being visible when there is chaos and invisible when things are going well. It's building one team at the top that speaks more or less with one voice. It's listening carefully much of the time, frequently speaking with encouragement, and reinforcing words with believable action. It's being tough when necessary, and it's the occasional naked use of power – or the "subtle accumulation of nuances, a hundred things done a little better," as Henry Kissinger once put it.

Good management occurs when one or more persons engage with others in such a way that managers and their constituents raise one another to higher levels of motivation and morality. Their purposes, which might have started out separate but related become focused. Good management is dynamic management in the sense that the managers throw themselves into a relationship with employees. In management process and thought emotions are an integral part of a manager's ability to motivate.

Questions to Ask

1) Do you think financial rewards are the most effective motivational tool?

2) Do you feel that fear of getting fired motivates people to be effective?

3) Is your reward and punishment system consistent with your goal setting?

4) Do you use one motivational strategy for all employees?

5) Do you reward not only good results but good efforts?

6) Are your employees interested in what they do?

7) Do your motivational techniques get the behavior started or can you count on your employees to repeat it even when you are not around?

8) Do your employees think of themselves as winners?

9) Do you arouse confidence in your followers?

10) Do you feel you adequately recognize people for their good work?

ACCOUNTABILITY

Clarifying Expectations

In the challenging macro-economic environment of today the non-performing employee has many reasons for not being able to deliver on the requirements of his job. Hence, the first stage in the process of holding people accountable is clarifying expectations. It is impossible to hold people accountable when it is not clear to them what it is that is expected of them. Making expectations clear is essential to measuring performance. If team members don't understand the manager's expectations, they can't meet them. But members of the group may have expectations of the manager too, so a clear understanding of all expectations is important. Some expectations – both the manager's and the team's are unrealistic or inappropriate but if they are not discussed, people become frustrated and exasperated when their needs aren't being met or when they are getting negative reviews without a knowledge of why.

The manager of a project management team was

frustrated that he was let down by his own team on a consistent basis. Deadlines that had been agreed upon were not being met. The service they provided was not always as fast and efficient as he would have liked. He was at times not updated and informed on important issues and situations. He realized that many of his expectations had been discussed in passing and had not been communicated clearly. It had seemed obvious to him that there was no need to hammer them home once they had been mentioned. He started to change his approach. When he had to set an expectation, he made certain that he addressed that expectation directly rather than as a casual comment. He also spent a few minutes talking about its importance. An important additional step was asking whether there was any reason his expectation could not be met. If there were any concerns he dealt with them there and then. At the end of the meeting he checked for commitment from his team to meeting expectations.

Another of his traits that needed to improve was that he was allowing deadlines to slide. His team had caught on to the fact that if he said "It is needed by tomorrow" they could count on having a week to get it completed – his expectations seemed to be flexible. He clarified to his team that he expected all deadlines to be met. This step of changing the way he presented his expectations and his response when they were not met increased the team's performance significantly.

Determine the consequences

A major part of the process of holding people

accountable is that they should be aware of the consequences of their actions. It is important to reach a mutual understanding about what follows when the desired outcomes are achieved or not achieved. Positive consequences may include rewards, such as appreciation, flexible schedule and an expanded scope of responsibilities or promotions. Negative consequences might be a reprimand or termination.

Dishing out negative consequences without a profound value foundation can be detrimental to the work environment and might impact employee morale adversely. On the other hand threatening people with dire consequences if they do not do what they are supposed to do can help overcome inertia and insubordination. A thing to keep in mind is that when people are made to work under duress the quality of the work is invariably questionable. Punishment produces compliance and certainly not zeal. Nor does it stir up creativity and innovation. A threat of negative consequences produces anxiety and anxiety hinders the flow of ideas that creativity demands.

If the constituents are given an understanding of what results are expected up-front and what criteria are used to judge their performance, they are best-positioned to evaluate themselves. Mostly the manager evaluates the performance, sometimes using criteria that he springs on the constituents at the end of a specified work period. Mostly it is a surprise to the constituents. Unless expectations are clarified up front people are justified in feeling bewildered by what they are being held accountable for.

If there is enough trust in the relationship the manager may involve his constituents in establishment of the standards against which they may be measured and allow them to measure their own performance. The employee's evaluation will be more complete and accurate, than the manager's evaluation could ever be. An individual knows his or her own innate strengths and shortcomings.

Everyone is Accountable

When the manager is emotionally secure and tries not to usurp all the power and knows how to create a buy-in everyone is a manager, each person has the responsibility for guiding the organization toward its future. Everyone has a contribution in keeping people aligned with the values. It is not only the manager's job. Of course, the whole point of delegating is that people take initiative. When we set free the manager within our constituents, people aim at fixing the structural problems instead of placing the blame on others. When something needs to be done, everyone feels compelled to do it – and will not wait to be asked.

But with the liberty to take initiative comes responsibility for our own actions. If each person is a manager, then each accepts the responsibilities of management. It's as simple as picking up a piece of paper from the floor. You could ignore it. But true managers don't wait for others to do something. They embrace the duty for making it happen.

Dealing with Mistakes

We all make Mistakes. Yet we're more than happy to point mistakes out in others but are rather displeased when someone points out one of ours. We acknowledge we are not perfect but criticism is hard to bear.

No one likes to be on the wrong end of criticism, or a complaint. None of us celebrates seeing the finger of responsibility point at us. Being told we've made a bad decision or performed below par stings the ego. Mistakes get made and complaints get lodged day after day. No one can be on the mark 100% of the time or able to satisfy everyone.

The first step is to create an environment where people are open to receiving constructive criticism and suggestions. An environment where it is accepted that to err is human. One surefire method of communicating this message is to acknowledge your own mistakes. Admitting your fault is the best way for shifting momentum when blame is being disseminated. Be the first to admit your fault. Take the opposite course - blame other people for a mistake made – and in a blink they'll start to contradict you. Any organization that is able to admit mistakes is encouraging creativity and encouraging a process of risk taking.

We should think twice before assigning blame to anyone. If the person who made the mistake knows how and why it happened and what needs to be done to avoid repetition nothing at all needs to be said. Allowing the person to save face might be the best way to deal with the situation as long as the person does not feel that you are not discussing the problem because you consider the mistake to be too trivial. After all, the only thing you want to do is create effective action that improves the place and makes it closer to your vision. And talking about who was to blame is not the purpose.

Blaming people always causes them to become defensive. People who have been on the wrong end of bitter criticism are much less likely to take risks or to be creative. Instantly the manager has made quiescent a significant part of that employee's potential.

Some managers have a propensity to point a finger and look for someone to blame when faced with a difficult situation. Those blamed walk around disheartened and discouraged. The person being blamed is dispirited and the ignominy of failure is like a shackle around his wrist making the next attempt to succeed more difficult. The blamed individual loses confidence and the mistake becomes a habit. The negative focus on assigning the blame saps the energy of the entire team.

In cultures of success managers bring problems to the fore as early as possible, appreciating that there will be no pointing the finger at each other after the fact. Postponing action not only prevents the manager and the team from getting the help required to solve the problem but also prevents people from openly coming face to face with what went wrong and learning from their mistakes. Managers can unwittingly create blame cultures if their reaction to bad news is not conducive to candidness.

In a culture of success, risk taking is considered an integral part of growth. Mistakes are seen as opportunities to learn. Recurring mistakes that comprise performance related challenges are handled positively but promptly. The manager does not wait for the formal review to offer feedback. Pats on the back for work done well are given separately from developmental performance feedback so that the positive oomph produced by acknowledgment is not watered down.

Being Nice vs. Holding people Accountable

I am all for being considerate however, there are occasions when striking a balance is essential. Something needs to be done when work takes second place to feelings. Managers who overuse this style avoid offering feedback on performance that could assist employees to improve. They tend to be too concerned about getting along with people often at the cost of the task at hand. This type of association has been found to drive down the environment rather than raise it. Stewing about whether they are liked or not, such managers' avoidance of confrontation can ruin a group by guiding it to failure. Management is not a popularity contest.

Such managers can easily feel lost, their overly thoughtful stance creating a circumstance where they are the last to learn of bad news. In crisis when people need clear commands to steer through intricate situations, oblivious managers - friendly though they may be - leave employees rudderless. Holding people accountable puts teeth into the management process. If there is no accountability, the sense of responsibility is gradually lost. People start blaming circumstances or others for their poor performance.

On the other hand, giving cruel feedback can be a swathe for pure competitive aggression - an assault disguised as helpfulness. Many managers use these opportunities to vent the anxiety and stress put on them by the strain of the job.

There is another thing the manager has to be careful of. The manager's message must not sound phony. If a manager acts insincerely or manipulatively the emotional radar of employees will sense the note of spuriousness and they will not trust that manager. The handling of such relationships in a culture of success, then, begins with genuineness: acting from authentic feelings and beliefs. Once managers have adjusted to their own values and vision then their relationship management skills let them relate in ways that generate productivity and resonance.

People with strong social skills are seldom mean-spirited but productive relationship management is affability with a purpose: moving people in the right direction, whether that's concurrence on a strategic plan or zeal about a new initiative.

That is why socially skilled managers have reverberation with a wide circle of people - and have a flair for finding common ground. They work under the hypothesis that nothing important gets accomplished alone. Such managers have a set of connections in place when the time for action comes. In a period of time when more and more work is done -by email or by phone- relationship building, ironically, becomes more essential than ever for the manager.

However, management does demand toughness - at times. A good manager always has an intrinsic sense of when to be forceful confronting someone directly about their deviation from expectations and when to be friendly and use less direct methods to guide and influence.

Management demands making decisions: Someone has to guide people as to what to do, hold people to their obligations and be precise about consequences. Consensus building and all the refinement in the world does not always do the job. Sometimes it comes down to plainly using the authority of one's position to get people to act.

A common fault in many managers is the failure to be emphatically firm when it is called for. One impediment to such assertiveness is inaction, as can happen when a

D. Atif

manager is more concerned with being well-liked than with getting the task done right, and so puts up with less than stupendous performance rather than confronting the situation. People who are uncomfortable with conflict or anger are also often disinclined to take a stand when it is called for.

Ineptitude here can surface in something as routine as failing to take charge in a meeting and so letting it wander rather than steering it straight to key agenda items.

A telling sign of a good manager is the ability to say 'no' decisively. Another is to set lofty expectations for performance or quality and be adamant that employees meet them.

If and when employees are unable to perform, the manager's task is to give feedback rather than let the lapse go unnoted. When someone constantly performs below expectations in spite of all efforts at supportive feedback and development, the issue has to be confronted directly.

Take the example of the manager who didn't set any regulation about meetings. The first meeting she ran, people straggled in late and weren't prepared. So when it happened a third time she put her foot down. She said, 'Ladies and gentlemen, I can't accept this behavior. I'm postponing this meeting for two days. Be on time and be prepared, or there'll be hell to pay.'

A timely use of controlled outbursts can be stirring as they can be a way to raise the temperature of the group. Teams tend to be most prolific in that middle zone between boredom and immobilizing angst. A moderate amount of anxiety, a sense of exigency, mobilizes us. Too little urgency and we are listless; too much and we are beleaguered.

This ability to be assertive and the ability to put your foot down deals with not only situations associated to management but also to daily life. The way you spend your time is a consequence of the way you view your priorities. If your priorities stem from a principled stance and a vision and if they are deeply rooted in your heart and mind, you will be able to set the priorities according to what is significant to you.

It is nearly not possible to say "no" if you don't have a larger "yes" aflame inside. Only when you have the mind and creativity to devise a unique program founded on principle to which you can say "yes" only then will you have adequate independent will power to say "no," with a smile, to the insignificant.

It isn't sufficient to set course by making decisions and then hoping that employees in the organization will have the incentive or skills to get there. In fact, where a lot of managers stumble is being overly sensitive about employees because it involves giving difficult face-to-face feedback and sometimes letting employees go. Some of the tough decisions taken in the 21st century do exhibit management edge that is based on solid business principles and sound value judgment. The decisions were based on the strength of the leader's convictions. The managers were keen to make decisions and to take actions when others would do nothing. They refused to let complexity stand in the way of acting on their deeply held values and beliefs.

Slash and Burn Managers

Being a good manager does not describe the petty despot

or the bully boss. And being tough is a tactic that comes into action only when other approaches have failed and not as a first response. If a manager's everyday style is severe and loud, then his ability to build rapport and influence people is wanting. In other words, unvarying toughness is a sign of weakness, not a sign of strong management ability.

The glorification of tough managers ignores the cost to the organization. Decisiveness in making difficult decisions is necessary but if that decision is carried out with callousness, the boss who did it will end up despised and a failure as a manager.

Having the capability to keep desire for power under control is a mark of the great manager. In good managers and executives, the drive of ambition is held in check by self-control, and a focus toward collective goals.

Slash and burn managers may be mistakenly thought to be leaders with effective managerial skills. But they are not because they only tear down organizations rather than building them up. The difference between good managers and bullies is that good managers are motivated to develop their organizations rather than to get more wealth for themselves or save their jobs. They are driven by a vision of organizational triumph rather than being driven by a search for personal glory. In fact, a major trait of good managers is that they exhibit strength of character and equanimity even in times of personal distress.

From time to time, Fortune produces a piece listing the 'Toughest bosses in Business." Some of them are good managers and are driven by principles, and are harsh at times because they know they have to for the benefit of the organization. Others are simply fools that confuse tyranny with leadership. The difference between them is that good managers are focused on seeing reality they value other people and go to great lengths to elucidate their actions and help others realize the difference between vindictiveness and holding people accountable. Managers with strength of character are esteemed not just by superiors but by employees working for them.

Managers have to look at the thinking processes and values of those in the group and compare them with their vision and make sure the employees in place are going to contribute to it and not be a hindrance in shaping that vision into actuality. Strength of character means being honest about what the organization requires from each and every employee and helping people but ultimately making a decision about whether a person can become a part of that vision or not.

The Contradiction

In spite of the evidence that excessively commanding bosses create a catastrophic discord most of us can name a rude, hard-hitting, tough boss who by all appearances characterizes the antithesis of resonance yet he seems to reap great results.

Managers with such huge egos typically have blinder-like fixation on immediate goals without regard for the long-term human/organizational costs of how they accomplish those goals. Too often the organizations they leave behind demonstrate signs of steroid abuse: pumped up for a concentrated period of time to show profitability but at the cost of the long-term human/economic resources critical to sustaining those profits.

In brief it is too easy to make an erroneous argument against the efficacy of holding people accountable in a balanced way by telling an anecdote about a tough manager whose business results seem good in spite of his coarseness. Such a naïve argument - that good managers succeed by being mean-spirited and pitiless (or in spite of it) can be made only in the absence of hard data about what kinds of management gets results.

A scientific study of managers begins by clearing away the fog, leveling the playing field to make efficient comparisons. A trade association commissioned a study of the management traits of CEOs and the business results of the companies they led. They tracked the results achieved by nineteen CEOs of insurance companies and divided them into two clusters-"outstanding" and "good"- on the basis of gauges such as their company's profitability and growth. Then they conducted intensive interviews to gauge the abilities that differentiated the outstanding CEOs from those who merely did an okay job.

The single talent that sets the most successful CEOs at a distance from others turned out to be a vital mass of emotional kindliness. The more successful CEOs spent the most amount of time coaching their senior executives cultivating personal relationships with them. When the company's CEO showed emotional kindliness, profits and sustained growth were maximum - significantly superior to organizations where CEOs lacked that sensitivity. It was discovered that handling an emotional situation required troubleshooting skills and being able to establish belief and rapport quickly and to convince and sell a recommendation.

On the other hand interpersonal incompetence in managers worsens everyone's performance: It creates bitterness and corrodes enthusiasm and dedication. A manager's strength or weakness in emotional kindliness can be measured in the retention or loss to the companies of the most talented personnel.

The importance of emotional kindliness increases, the higher you go in the organization. Emotional kindliness makes the crucial difference between mediocre managers and the best. The best managers show considerably greater strengths in a range of emotional skills, among them power of persuasion, team leadership, self-confidence, and accomplishment drive. On average, close to 90 percent of success in leadership was attributable to emotional proficiency.

Criticize Respectfully

Sometimes holding people accountable comes down to criticizing people. Managers use euphemisms such as "feedback" and "suggestions" to get around the potential conflict. But it must be remembered that employees long for feedback, yet too many managers are not sufficiently expert in giving any. In Asia and Scandinavia there is an implied prohibition against expressing criticism openly. In a study of the consequences of performance feedback on self-assurance, some students were praised, criticized, or got no feedback on how they performed in a simulation of problem solving. They had been informed that their efforts would be contrasted with how well others had done on the same task. Those who heard nothing about how they did experienced as great a blow to their self-assurance as those who were criticized. The good manager gives explicit information about what is wrong, combined with curative feedback and a positive expectation of the person's ability to improve. By contrast, the worst way to provide feedback is in a fit of rage, when the effect is inevitably a character attack.

If there is one place where showing emotional kindliness is important it is while criticizing constituents. Firstly, if it is a one off mistake nothing needs to be said. If the mistake is made often enough and there is an urgent need then something needs to be done. If after thoughtful deliberation, you decide you have to thrash out a situation criticize respectfully. Let the person being criticized save face at all costs. This may denote calling attention to the person's gaffes indirectly or asking questions as opposed to giving orders. Or it may mean postponing some criticism till another day. Or mentioning some mistake you made communicating that no one is perfect. However, whatever method you choose to do it in, the aim is the same: be gentle, play down and do not attack. Make the faults seem easy to correct. Present complaints in the shape of requests and suggestions mapping the course for recovery for the person being criticized.

Questions to Ask

1) In your office environment is there an understanding that mistakes are a part of life?

2) Do you readily admit fault yourself?

3) How do you react when problems arise and mistakes come to light?

4) Do you show composure even in times of personal distress?

5) Do you criticize respectfully?

6) Do you argue, belittle or shout?

7) Do you make faults seem easy to correct?

8) Do you make certain constituents get feedback?

9) Do you clarify your expectations of them with your constituents?

10) Do you delegate authority throughout the organization?

DEDICATION TO THE CUSTOMER

In one form or another every business part takes in something resembling a sale and the company and the customer transact. That an organization should be close to its customers seems a predictable enough statement. Yet, in spite of all the lip service paid to the subject the customer is considered a little more than a nuisance in today's corporate culture in Canada.

The market leaders, however, have what we call a dedication to the customer. You can't help noticing it when you find a company that has it, and yet you can't immediately put your fingers on what it is. Dedication to the customer is expressed in people's attitudes and behaviors. It's what separates the winners from the losers in the race for market leadership. Few market-leading companies - in fact, have achieved or retained their position without a palpable culture that aligns precisely with their commitment to customers.

Dedication to the customer in practice takes on hard

edges that are easily recognizable. Walk around a market-leading company and stop some rank–and-file employees in the hallway. Ask them what success means in their company and what makes them proud to be there. They'll probably talk about success in terms of value created for customers. Their pride derives from being able to touch their customers – directly or indirectly, but always tangibly. People throughout these organizations know that they can make a difference to buyers and users of their products and services. Keep talking with the employees of these companies, and you'll hear some deeply held beliefs that, in one way or another, capture two notions: First, customer value is the ultimate measure of one's work performance. Second, improving value (and the pace at which this is done) is the measure of one's success. Once absorbed into the fabric of a company, this credo assures that all employees engage their heads, their hands, and - in a sign of pure commitment - their hearts in going the extra distance for the customer.

Customer dedication differs among companies pursuing different value disciplines. In operationally focused companies what stands out is employees' dedication to total dependability. Employees are proud that customers can count on them that they're rock-solid in following up on what they promise. They want to be measured by how well they meet customer's expectations.

Using the Mission Statement

Generally an organization's own mission statement gets some attention and focus but to the average employee it does not mean much especially a few weeks into the job and a valuable motivational tool goes to waste. The reason for this lack of interest is that the average employee has had no input in the process. I suggest that in service oriented organizations the mission statement should establish the predominant focus on the customer relationship and rather than all the attention given to the corporate mission statement a mission statement for each department ought to be written by each department in line with the corporate mission statement. Just because each member of the department would have contributed in the writing of the mission statement it would mean a lot more to the employees and they will be a lot more motivated to back it up with actions.

Attention to the little things

If we could set up quantifiable measures to evaluate each employee's efforts in doing the little things like smiling, like thanking the other person, like being more friendly to the customer and building a closer relationship we would be a lot more effective in making the employees more motivated to do all of these things rather than the only time their people skills are brought into question is when a customer complains. Now a left brain sort of a person might say these touchy feely things have no place in a profit-oriented organizational structure but this is the most important ingredient for any business organization especially a customer service oriented one.

I will give you an example of what motivates people to go that extra mile and make sure that the customer's experience is more than satisfactory. A little while ago a Bank of Montreal employee did something right and Mike Kooksy the Area Manager stopped by at her cubicle and complimented her in spite of his busy schedule. That really motivated her to go that extra mile. So my point is we need to make our employees happier and take notice when they do something right rather than to notice when they do something wrong as much as possible and tangible revenue based results will automatically follow, otherwise we will just be hacking at the leaves and never deal with the roots of the problem.

The good news from the market leading companies is the extent to which, and the intensity with which, the customers intrude into every aspect of the business – sales, manufacturing, research, accounting. A simple message permeates the atmosphere. Build a solid relationship with the customer.

Being pushed around by the Customer

The market leaders are better listeners. They get a benefit from market closeness and their real innovation comes from the market.

Proctor & Gamble was one of the first consumer goods company to put the toll-free number on all its packaging. In its 1979 annual report, P & G says it got 200,000 calls on that 800 number, calls with customer ideas or complaints. P & G responded to every one of those calls and the calls were summarized monthly for board meetings. Insiders report that the 1-800number is a major source of product improvement ideas.

The best companies are pushed around by their customers, and they love it. Who in Levi Strauss invented the original Levi's jean? Nobody did. In 1873, for $68 levi's obtained the right to market steel-riveted jeans from one of its users Jacob Youphes, a Nevada buyer of levi's denim.

Commitment

In observing the market leaders and specifically the way they interact with customers, what I found most striking was the consistent presence of commitment. A seemingly unjustifiable over-commitment to some form of quality, reliability, or service. Being customer-oriented doesn't mean that market leaders are incompetent when it comes to technological or cost performance. But they do seem more driven by their direct orientation to their customers than by technology or by a desire to be the low-cost producer. Take IBM, for example. It is hardly far behind the times, but most observers will agree that it hasn't been a technology leader for decades. Its dominance rests on its commitment to service.

Service, quality, reliability is a strategy aimed at loyalty and long-term revenue stream growth (and maintenance). The trick is to continue to listen to the customer. As Freddy Heineken puts it, "I must keep telling my marketing people not to make the (beer) bottle too elaborate with gold foil or fancy labels. Otherwise, the housewife will be too intimidated to take it off the supermarket shelf."

Of course, in an absolute sense, one can commit too much to service and quality. But if yes is the answer absolutely, then I would say no directionally. That is, just as there are "too many" champions at Google and "too many" divisions at J&J, according to rational analysis, almost every one of our service-oriented institutions does "overspend" on service, quality and reliability. David Ogilvy said "In the best institutions promises are kept no matter what the cost in agony." It holds for advertising, for computers, for amusement rides.

The impossible becomes almost possible in the market leaders. Is a 100 percent quality or service program possible? Most would guffaw at the thought. But the answer is yes and no. Statistically, it's no. In a big company, the law of large numbers ensures that there will be defects and breached service standards now and again. On the other hand a friend at American Express reminds me, "If you don't shoot for 100%, you are tolerating mistakes. You'll get what you ask for." Thus it is possible to be aggrieved by failure, any failure, despite the volume. Freddy Heineken says bluntly, "I consider a bad bottle of Heineken to be a personal insult to me." Even with high standards, companies can get lax if just an occasional failure in quality and service is considered tolerable. A Digital executive summarizes: "It's the difference between day and night. One is the mindset that says, 'Doing it right is the only way.' The other treats the customer as a statistic. Do you want to be part of the population struck by 'failure within tolerance'?"

The customer orientation is by definition a way of "tailoring"- a way of finding a particular niche where you are better at something than anybody else. A very large share of the companies I looked at is superb at dividing their customer base into numerous segments so it can provide tailored products and service. In doing so, of course, they take their products out of the commodity category, and then they charge more for them. I find five fundamental attributes of those companies that are close to the customer through niche strategies: 1) astute technology manipulation, (2) pricing skill, (3) better segmenting, (4) a problem-solving orientation, and (5) a willingness to spend in order to discriminate.

Regimenting Customer Service

Even though aligning the employees with the profound values of the company and helping them see the clear connection between the loyalty of the customer and their own well being is important micro managing in this regard can be counterproductive. Some of the tools that regiment employees' interaction too much with the customer tend not to work.

For example, employees of a major bank in downtown Toronto were made to adopt a set of practices in dealing with the customer called 'Cuber's Code'. Instead of improving the quality of customer service it had the opposite effect of making employees feel unconfident, incompetent and feel that they lack basic human creativity. Their smiles and interaction with the client seemed increasingly not insincere. It increased employee turnover because the employees spent their time fearing if they were leaving out any of the steps dictated by the Cuber's Code.

In my opinion the real problem is to get a greater buy in from all the employees in having a high standard of customer service. Some methods that we can use to get a greater buy in from the employees are getting them to write out a mission statement, making customer service as quantifiable as possible and encouraging any positive behavior.

Questions to Ask

1) Do you have a mission statement written by each department for that department in line with the corporate mission statement?

2) Do you make an effort to make customer satisfaction as quantifiable as possible?

3) Do you take notice when someone does anything right or only when someone does anything wrong?

4) Do your employees know that you can make a difference to the end user of the product?

5) Do your employees want to be measured by how satisfied the customer?

6) Can you spend too much on service?

7) Are you committed to quality and reliability?

8) Can your customers get your message across to you?

THE ABILITY TO TAKE RISKS AND MAKE DECISIONS

The passionate search for opportunities beyond what is the status quo comes with a certain degree of risk. It requires creativity, innovation and more than all else guts. Good managers are open to stepping into untested waters and accepting the risks that accompany all experiments. The first step is emancipating one's self of psychologically self-imposed limitations. Innovation is imperative to the healthy growth of the organization. Without constant innovation in products and services an organization will plateau. We need to look outside the existing way of doing things if we're to be innovative. Here a manager who is respectful of the past but is confident enough to take the plunge into the unpredictable without caring about other people's opinions triumphs.

A little bit of a 'do not care' attitude is essential because an integral part of risk taking is that the manager puts himself and others at risk. In fact not only that he takes risks himself but also encourages others to take risks as well. In fact one of the most glaring differences between the manager and the bureaucrat is the good manager's inclination to encourage risk taking, to encourage others to step out into the unknown rather than to play it safe. He builds risk taking into the goal setting process. He sets goals that are higher than current levels, but not so high that people feel only frustration and are so burnt by the risk taking process that they are too shy to try again. Good managers raise the bar gradually and offer coaching and training to build skills that help people get over each new level of risk taking.

Experimentation

When the good manager is uncertain about the effect of a new idea he experiments with it first. Consumer product companies try out a new product in limited locations before launching it in all markets, for example. The good manager does not wait till he has a perfect product or process before trying it out. He realizes that the window of opportunity can close very quickly.

However, a thorough evaluation of the processes involved in exploring a new opportunity can be very useful in limiting the massive uncertainty involved in risk taking as well. The most important part of the testing process is establishing ways of quantifying the outcome. Once you have established ways of quantifying the outcomes, conduct pretests with your control groups, run the experiment, and measure the results. While the costs of research evaluation are often great the learning is usually worth the expense.

An essential part of being a manager is to experiment with new approaches to old problems. Yet innovation is always risky. They realize that we may make a mistake when we try something new. Prudent managers recognize failure as a necessary fact of the innovative life. They not only reward successes but the quality and the sincerity of the effort as well. Instead of punishing people for failure they encourage them to try again. When the instinctive and human thing to do would be to fix blame for mistakes, they learn from them. Instead of becoming more controlling and micro managing they continue to encourage flexibility. That flexibility comes from an inherent strength of the good manager where ideas flow freely.

Rationality in the business world today does not value experimentation and abhors mistakes. This leads to inaction and a desire to make perfect decisions. This inaction and search for guarantees frequently confronts organizations with having to make eventually one big decision. Giant product development groups analyze and analyze until years have gone by and they've designed themselves into one home-run product. Meanwhile successful organizations amid a hotbed of experimentation, have proceeded chaotically, and induced ten or more new products each during the same period. There is one person's gut feeling behind those almost chaotic decisions; the manager's.

Provide a safe Environment

Not only does the good manager have the strength to take risks himself he creates an environment that encourages risk taking. The constituents are certain that if they take risks in the best interest of the company they will not be punished. Gene Calvert author of High Wire Management offers a number of specific actions that managers can take to make others feel safe:

1) Verifying whether people feel ready for the new or challenging assignment, asking them how best to support their management of the risks involved, and encouraging them to ask for help whenever they need it.

2) Holding informal face-to-face updates sessions

3) Resist the well-meaning tendency to snoop

4) Provide others the flexibility to handle any risk in their own way - unless this sets them up to fail in ways you find unaffordable or that are detrimental to them

5) It is also important to keep your word about not punishing people when they've done their best under the circumstances, regardless of how the situation turns out.

In making it safe for people to experiment, you must also make sure it's safe for them to challenge authority. Weaker managers are far too trigger-happy to interpret healthy disagreement as mutiny. It is only a genuinely good manager who does not take every suggestion contrary to his own opinion as a direct blow to his self-esteem. So if you want people to act with a shared sense of commitment and urgency, be sure they feel safe in challenging authority.

At the basis of that feeling of security and the resulting

zeal in employees is their relationship with their manager. They feel secure enough in their relationship to explore new territories and take on fresh challenges. In this way, trust is the most important ingredient in organizational development. The irony is that people cannot take risks unless they feel that they will not be unfairly treated, embarrassed, harassed, or harmed by taking some action. When we feel safe we do not become defensive because our self-esteem is not being threatened.

Vision-Based Risk taking

When managers have a vision that they feel driven to pursue they realize they have to be willing to take risks in order to strive for it. One of the reasons good managers are willing to take risks is that they recognize there is a price for not initiating too. President John F. Kennedy said, "There are risks and costs to a program of action, but they are far less than the long-range risks and costs of comfortable inaction."

Good managers are often despised and viewed negatively exactly because they take risks and show initiative. They have a vision that others don't, and in trying to show others why their vision is right and why others should follow them, they run the risk of offending some people. But good managers know that life isn't a popularity contest. They do whatever they believe to be right and have enough self confidence to be 'wrong' when everyone else is 'right'.

Paralysis through Analysis

The reason behind the absence of effective risk taking in many North American companies is the over reliance on planning. This over reliance on planning would appear to eliminate risks but also, unfortunately eliminates action. The problem is not that companies ought not to plan. They absolutely should plan. The problem is that planning becomes an end in itself. The plan becomes the truth, and the data that don't fit the preconceived plan are ignored or the search for the perfect plan with the perfect results takes so much time that many opportunities are lost.

Organizations and managers who follow Fredrick Taylor's school of scientific management seem to believe in analyzing everything. They believe in big decisions through good market research, discounted cash-flow analysis, and big budgeting. If a little is good, then more must be better, so apply things like discounted cash flow to risky investments like research and development. Use budgeting as a model for long-range planning. Make forecasts. Set hard numerical targets on the basis of those forecasts. Produce fat planning volumes whose main content is numbers.

They believe that if we get the incentives right productivity will follow. If we give people big, straightforward monetary incentives to do right and work smart, the productivity problem will go away. Over-reward the top performers. Weed out the 30 to 40 percent dead wood that don't want to work. This kind of approach gives too little credit to the power of personalities involved. They believe that if you can read the financial statements, you can manage anything. The people, the products, and the services are simply those resources you have to align to get good financial results.

This sort of rationality does not explain most of what makes some companies work with one formula and the same formula not being successful in another company. For one, the analytical component has an in-built conservative bias. One common impact of excessive planning in organizations is an over emphasis on cost reduction. This obsession with cost instead of quality and value becomes expensive in the long run. It leads to patching up old products rather than fooling with untidy new products. It quietly stifles creativity and innovation. All productivity issues are solved through focus on products and processes rather than revitalization of the work force or change in management techniques. A hidden flaw in the analytic approach to decision making is that people analyze what can be most readily analyzed.

As Harvard's John Steinbruner observes, "If quantitative precision is demanded, it is gained, in the current state of things, only by so reducing the scope of what is analyzed that most of the important problems remain external to the analysis." This leads to fixation on the cost side of the equation often.

The Analytic approach's extensive emphasis on planning leads to a philosophy that is less than dynamic. To be narrowly rational is often to be negative. Peter Drucker gives a good description of the baleful influence of management's analytic bias: "professional management today sees itself often in the role of a judge who says 'yes' or 'no' to ideas as they come up… A top management that believes its job is to sit in judgment will inevitably veto the new idea. It is always 'impractical.' John Steinbrener makes a similar point commenting on the role of staffs in general: "It is inherently easier to develop a negative argument than to advance a constructive one." George Gilder in *Wealth and Poverty* says, "Creative thought requires an act of faith." Going back to the laying out of railroads he says "when they were built they could hardly be justified in economic terms."

The dominant culture in business enterprises demands punishment for a mistake, no matter how useful, small or invisible. This is especially ironic because the ancestor of today's business rationality was called scientific management. Experimentation is the fundamental tool of science: if we experiment successfully, by definition, we will make many mistakes.

There is no simple method for determining the appropriate level of risk in a project. We must weigh pros and cons, costs and benefits, potential losses versus potential gains. Realizing that one person's challenge is another's routine activity, we must factor in the present skill levels of the team members and the demands of the task. But even if we could compute risk to a negligible level, every innovation would still expose us to some uncertainty. Perhaps the healthiest thing we can do is evaluate whether what we can learn is worth the cost. And our ability to grow and learn under stressful, risk-abundant situations is highly based on how we respond to change.

The Strength to Fail

A special trait of the good manager is a substantial tolerance for failure. James Burke, Johnson & Johnson's CEO, says one of J&J's tenets is that "you've got to be willing to fail." Emerson Charles Knight argues: "You need the ability to fail. You cannot innovate unless you are willing to accept mistakes." Tolerance for failure is a very specific part of the excellent company culture – and that lesson comes directly from the top. Constituents have to make lots of tries and consequently suffer some failures or the organization won't learn and grow.

One important observation about failure: it's a lot less punishing with regular dialogue. The big failures that really leave scars are usually the ones in which a project was allowed to go on without serious guidance. Such catastrophes rarely occur at the no-holds-barred communication environment at the companies that succeed. The exchange is frank and honest. You can't hide the really bad news, and you don't want or need to. You know you will not be persecuted for trying.

Perhaps the most impressive and memorable quality of good managers is the way they respond to failure. Like a tightrope aerialist – whose life was at stake each time he walks the tight rope – good managers put all their energies into their task. They simply don't think about failure, they don't even use the word, relying on such synonyms as a "glitch," or an "error". They never use the term failure. As one of them said, "If I have an Art form of management, it is to make as many mistakes as quickly as I can in order to learn." One recalled Harry Truman's famous maxim, "Whenever I make a bum decision, I just go out and make another one."

For a lot of people, the word "failure" carries with it finality, the absence of movement characteristic of a dead thing, to which the automatic human reaction is helpless discouragement. But for the successful manager, failure is a beginning, the springboard to hope.

The tension here, integrated by these managers, is

that of failure versus learning. While we can't say that they exactly hailed failure, they certainly seemed to profit from it. They used the energy springing from paradox to reach higher goals. Almost every "false step" was regarded as an opportunity and not as the end of the world. They were convinced that they could learn – and, more importantly, that their organizations could learn – how to succeed at whatever they undertook as their vision.

The good news for initiators is that they make things happen. The bad news is that they make lots of mistakes. IBM founder Thomas J Watson recognized that when he remarked, "The way to succeed is to double your failure rate."

Even though initiating managers experience more failure, they don't let it bother them. They remain undeterred. The greater the potential is the greater the chance for failure. US Senator Robert Kennedy summed it up: "Only those who dare to fail greatly can ever achieve greatly." If you want to achieve great things as a manager, you must be willing to initiate and put yourself on the line.

Failure can be costly. For the individual who leads a failed project, it can mean a blow to his career aspirations or even a lost job. For an adventurous entrepreneur it can mean the loss of personal assets. For mountain climbers and other physical adventurers, lives are at risk.

Success does not breed success. It breeds failure. It is failure which breeds success. Failure plays an important role in success. Recall the times when you tried to learn a new game or a new sport. We know from our own life experiences that nothing is ever done perfectly the first time we try - not in sports, not in games, not in school, and most certainly not in organizations.

My point isn't to promote failure for failure's sake, of

course. I don't advocate for a moment that failure ought to be the objective of any endeavor. Instead, I advocate learning. Managers don't look for someone to blame when mistakes are made in the name of innovation. Instead they ask, "What can be learned from that experience?" Indeed, consider the very shape of most learning curves. Whether tracking our own performance or some new product, process or service, these curves invariably show performance going down before it goes up. Learning doesn't go up in the absence of mistakes.

Encouraging the Risk Takers

Every organization should find unique ways of honoring its innovators. Make sure to reward good attempts, not just successes. Well-intentioned attempts that don't work out are just as important as those that do. Many, if not most, innovations fail. If people are going to continue to contribute new ideas, they need to see that failure doesn't result in banishment.

The Risk of Change

Encourage people to see change as full of possibilities. As I've discussed, this requires making people feel safe and reducing the costs of failure. But beyond this, people are unlikely to show commitment to making new solutions work if they don't fully understand the issues and challenges in the first place. For the success of the change process develop a personal stake in the idea's success for all constituents. Put yourself in the other person's shoes and speak to the question. Appeal to the "What's in it for me?" mentality. Make certain that people see the benefits. And then be the first one to take the plunge. Lead by example. Encourage others to take risks by doing so yourself. Showing others that you're willing to take risks is essential to getting others to do the same.

Out of the uncertainty and chaos of change, managers articulate a new vision of the future that pulls the organization together. Through their efforts managers show how accepting the present challenge will actually help shape a better tomorrow. This is critical to commitment levels of constituents, since we need to believe that we're dedicating ourselves to the creation of a noble and meaningful future. We must feel that what we've committed ourselves to is worthy of our best efforts

It's altogether too easy to put down new ideas: "It's not in the budget." "The competition is too strong." "It'll never work." "We've never done that before." Too often, write Robert Kriegel and Louis Patler in *If it Ain't Broke...Break it!* People cling to the familiar and play it safe when confronted with change by responding like firefighters after the fact when the organization has lost its momentum. In order to move us out of our comfort zones, leaders should instead be on the lookout for ways to eliminate fire hosing. Ideas don't appear magically, fully created and ready to implement. They almost always require nurturing. If, as is usually the case, ideas that sound strange are rejected or ridiculed, two things generally happen:

Potentially good ideas are lost.

People stop offering ideas.

Question of physical safety provide dramatic emphasis in the question of trust. Yet emotional safety is no less significant. At Delphi Solutions, a medium-sized telecom equipment provider outside of Toronto, it's no longer difficult or threatening to convey ideas upward – thanks to increased accessibility. They've removed many of the physical demarcations between workers and management, and the management group is spending more of its time in the main floor than in its offices. Indeed, both groups seem quite comfortable in one another's work areas. When one of the Salesmen had an idea about changing the sales process he took it directly to the Vice President Kevin Watson. He listened; the plan was established.

Kevin Watson makes it a point to be visible: "I want it to be easy for people to talk with me. Initially it's often chitchat. But as people become more familiar and comfortable with me, the talk becomes more personal, and I learn about the things they really care about. And one of the things we care about in common is making this business a success." What Kevin demonstrates is that when people know us as individuals they are more likely to trust us. And when constituents trust us, they feel safe with us and when they feel safe with us, they are more likely to take risks with us.

Examples such as these and the research make it clear that shared trust or lack thereof is a significant determinant of managerial problem-solving effectiveness. Further, the more we trust those making decisions in an organization, the more satisfied we are with our level of participation in the process. In organizations in which mutual trust does not exist, people are cautious, less open, less satisfied, less influential, more distant, and more inclined to leave at the first available opportunity.

If we are reliable and others know they can count on us, then our words and actions have greater power to influence them. If we demonstrate that we take their interests genuinely to heart, they will trust us to guide and manage. People will be less suspicious and better able to deal with legitimate differences. On all fronts, developing the trust of their diverse constituents is critical to managers.

Only those managers who act boldly in times of crisis and change are willingly followed. This disregard for caution is the good manager's forte.

From Stress to Strength

Organizations can help their members cope more effectively with stress of taking risks by creating an environment that develops hardiness. In this regard organizations can build commitment by offering more rewards than punishments. They can build a sense of control by choosing tasks that are challenging but within the person's skill level. They can build an attitude of challenge by encouraging people to see change as full of possibilities.

There are two important implications for managers from this work on being strong when faced with stress. First, people can't lead if they aren't psychologically hardy. No one will follow someone who avoids stressful events and won't take decisive action. Second, even if managers are personally tough they cannot enlist and retain others if they don't create an atmosphere that promotes psychological hardiness. People won't remain long with a cause that distresses them. They need to share their manager's focus, control and risk taking ability. In short, they need to believe that they can overcome challenges if they're to accept the process of transformation. Managers must create the conditions that make all of that possible.

Struggles and hardships have a way of making us come face to face with who we really are and we're capable of becoming.

Name any top manager chances are that the catalyst for that person's crowning achievement was some risky venture. Only challenge produces the opportunity for greatness.

In the process of transformation people and their organizations live with a high degree of ambiguity. Innovation upsets the stability we've worked hard to establish; it throws off our equilibrium. As Meg Wheatley points out in *Leadership and the New Science*, "The things we fear most in organizations - fluctuations, commotions, imbalances" are also the main source of innovation. But how do we get from the challenging parts of this process to the empowering parts? Fortunately, there are some steps we can take for making this painful process more palatable.

As we have seen, managers and constituents alike need psychological hardiness to cope well with the risks and the failures of innovation and the challenge of change. In fact, strong management is needed more during times of uncertainty than in times of stability otherwise constituents might end up feeling rudderless. Good managers master change and they master uncertainty seizing the imperative to act. They know that action and flexibility are required to bring people through these times.

The Power to be Flexible

People have a tendency to resort to self-pity when they're hurt by events in their corporate or personal lives. But those who rise through adversity don't allow themselves to be resentful, bitter, or alienated. Instead they become engaged, involved and committed and inspire others.

People are inspired by those who take initiative, risk personal safety for the sake of a cause. Only those who act boldly in times of crisis and change are going to succeed. Without courage there can be no hope - and little chance of survival in today's highly volatile economic and social situations. No one can accurately predict what will happen next. Those supple enough to adapt to the shifting conditions will succeed.

Yet flexibility can increase stress on the system and must be balanced with extreme discipline. Both are essential if we want to experiment and take risks. Everyone must have a total sense of personal responsibility and commitment. True freedom is learning discipline first, and then acting with it.

Are you afraid to acknowledge fear?

While managers must act decisively under urgent and uncertain conditions, they must also acknowledge the fear and doubt that people feel as they face the unknown. Managers have a responsibility when people feel alienated, frustrated and fail. Those Managers who take the time to listen, support, and communicate will find it easier to mobilize action in the face of such feelings. Good managers enable their constituents to move through fear and risk and find the new opportunities that inevitably arise in times of tremendous change. Napolean used to say to his army before battle that I am aware that you are afraid but just pretend to be brave and that is how you will behave in battle.

With an attitude of psychological hardiness, good managers can turn the potential turmoil and stress of innovation into an adventure. There are ways to establish a climate in which people can take charge of change and turn uncertainty into an opportunity to experiment, take risks, and learn from the accompanying mistakes.

Managers see change as an opportunity to innovate. They venture outside the constraints of normal routine and experiment with creative and risky solutions. Their first act during times of adversity is to create a climate in which organizational members can also accept the challenge of change and act freely.

The Risk of making Decisions

Good managers strip out everything that does not create their vision, which means first facing reality, often alone and against the stinging scorn of those they work with. It means having the courage to act, even if it means venturing into the unknown or cutting so sharply it bleeds.

Napolean said "Nothing is more difficult and therefore more precious, than to be able to decide." The Frenchman definitely made some major calls, such as invading Russia. Decisions like that either leave you wearing an emperor's crown or leave you in pajamas on Elba.

If there's one thing we humans hate, it is uncertainty. The Persians had an approach to decision making which many corporate decision makers could make use of today. Herodotus recorded around 430 B.C.: "If an important decision is to be made, they discuss it when they are drunk. The following day, the master of the house submits their decision for reconsideration when they are sober. If they still approve it, it is adopted; if not, it is abandoned. Conversely, any decision they make when they are sober is reconsidered afterwards when they are drunk."

Business is a bad hiding place for people afraid of making decisions. Strategies, careers, companies – they are all products of decisions and decision making. The quality of your decisions is what makes you valuable. And the hardest ones roll uphill: A CEO's job, it's been said is to make decisions that can't be delegated.

There is no greater risk than making a decision. Start with the Latin word 'decidere'. It means literally to "cut off." Decisions force us to foreclose other opportunities – jobs not taken, strategies never attempted, options not pursued. Would that sales gig in Calgary have worked out better? You'll never know.

Most of us will do just about anything to avoid uncertainty. We might postpone decisions endlessly or, like ripping off a Band-Aid, pull the trigger all at once. Making a call takes guts. It means inviting uncertainty into your home. Uncertainty is a creepy houseguest, but not your captor. If surmounting your anxiety about uncertainty is the first step, the second step is letting go of your inner search for the perfect decision because there is no such thing as a perfect decision. Even if you had all the information in the world and a hangar full of supercomputers, you'd still get some wrong.

But there is a big difference between a wrong decision

and a bad decision. A wrong decision is picking the right hand when the prize is actually in the left hand. It's a lousy result but the fault lies with the method. A bad decision is launching the space shuttle Challenger when Morton Thiokol's engineers predict a nearly 100% chance of catastrophe. The method in this case is no method at all.

The distinction is important, because it separates outcomes, which you can't control from process which you can. Wrong decisions are an inevitable part of life and are acceptable risks. But bad decisions are unforced errors. They are eminently avoidable.

Risk Taking from the Gut

Risk Taking is one place where the good managers muster up all their strength of character and more than anything else choose to believe in themselves. Of sixty highly successful entrepreneurs connected with companies having revenues ranging from $2 million to $400 million, just one said his business decisions were made using the classic decision tree method - and even he added that his final decisions were still made intuitively. The others all either used their feelings to confirm (or disconfirm) a rational analysis or let their emotions guide them at the outset and subsequently looked for data or a rationale that supported their gut hunch.

The ability to read such subjective currents has primal roots in evolution. The brain areas involved in gut feelings are far more ancient than the thin layers of the neo cortex, the centers for rational thought that enfold the very top of the brain. Hunches start much deeper in the brain.

They are a function of the emotional centers that ring the brain stem atop the spinal cord - most particularly this almond-shaped structure called the amygdale and its connected neural circuitry. This web of connectivity, sometimes called the extended amygdale, stretches up to the brain's executive center in the prefrontal lobes, just behind the forehead.

The brain stores different aspects of an experience in different areas - the source of a memory is encoded in one zone, the sights and sounds and smells in other areas, and so on. Every experience that we have an emotional reaction to, no matter how subtle seems to be encoded in the amygdale.

As the repository for everything we feel about what we experience, the amygdale constantly signals us with this information. When we have a preference that is a message from the amygdale and via the amygdale's related circuitry, particularly nerve pathways that run into the viscera, we can have a somatic response-literally, a "gut feeling" to the choices we face.

This capacity, like other elements of intelligence, can grow stronger with the accumulating experiences life brings us. The classic term for this strengthening of our guiding sensibility is Wisdom. People who ignore or discount messages from the repository of life's wisdom do so at their peril.

One of the causes of what lead us into this financial crisis was the lack of the use of this old fashioned ability in today's highly mechanized and web-driven financial institutions. Credit managers in the past 'sensed' when a deal might go bad even if the numbers looked fine.

Studies at Harvard suggest that people can sense intuitively in the first thirty seconds of an encounter what basic impression they will have of the other person after fifteen minutes - or half a year. For instance, when people watch just thirty-second snatches of teachers giving a lecture, they can assess each teacher's proficiency with about 80 percent accuracy.

Intuition and gut feeling bespeak the capacity to sense messages from our internal store of emotional memory - our own reservoir of wisdom and judgment and these are the two most important elements of any decision to take risks. This ability also lies at the heart of self-awareness, and self awareness is a vital skill.

In the rush and pressure of our work days, our minds are pre-occupied by the stream of thought - planning the next thing, immersion in our present task, preoccupation with things undone. It takes a mental pause to become sensitive to the murmur of mood - a moment we rarely take. Our feelings are always with us but we are seldom with them. Emotions have their own agenda and timetable but our rushed lives give them no air time- and so they go underground. All of this mental pressure crowds out a quieter inner voice that offers an inner rudder of conviction we could use to navigate through life and risky situations.

Self-awareness can be cultivated to include intuition in the risk taking decision making process without letting the mind get in the way. Sometimes all it takes is to take time out to 'do nothing.' Doing nothing productively means not only not working, but also not filling the time with idle time wasters. Instead it means putting aside for the time being all other goal-oriented activities and doing something that opens our minds to a deeper, quieter sensibility.

Unless we remain in touch with the inner self we risk drifting away from our guiding values. Personal values are not lofty abstractions, but intimate credos that we may never quite articulate in words so much as feel. Our values translate into what has emotional power or resonance for us, whether negative or positive.

Self-awareness serves as an inner barometer, gauging whether what we are doing is, indeed worthwhile. Feelings give the essential reading. If there is discrepancy between action and value, the result will be uneasiness in the form of guilt or shame, deep doubts or nagging second thoughts or remorse.

Choices made in keeping with this inner rudder, on the other hand, are energizing and risks taken in the process have a refreshing conviction. They not only feel right but maximize the attention and energy available for pursuing them. While average workers are content to take on whatever project they were assigned, superior performers think about what project would be invigorating to work on, which person would be stimulating to work under, which personal idea would make a good project. They know intuitively what they do best and enjoy - and what they do not. Their performance excels because they were able to make choices that keep them focused and energized.

Do Not Overuse Compromise in Taking Risks and Making Decisions

Good managers do not overuse compromise. Compromise might sound like a positive team practice, but it can be the most direct route to mediocrity. Compromise occurs when there is an attempt to create a solution that has something in it for everyone, and it is a common decision-making pitfall. The process of compromise usually ends up watering down a decision on a challenge to be undertaken until its weak enough that no one can object. Unfortunately, neither can anyone get excited about the challenge.

Questions To Ask

1) Do you believe that innovation is necessary for the growth of the organization?

2) Do you build risk taking into your employees' goal setting process?

3) While experimenting do you wait for the product or process to be perfect   before you try it out?

4) While experimenting do you make sure the results of your experiment are quantifiable?

5) Do you provide a safe environment for your constituents to take risks regardless of how the situation turns out?

6) Is it acceptable to you to offend some people who do not share your vision or initiative?

7) Does failure in an experiment make you hesitant to try again?

8) Is your view of change positive or negative?

9) Do you find yourself postponing many decisions?

10) Do you consistently make decisions by committee?

TRANSFORMATIONAL LEADERSHIP: THE LEADER'S BIGGEST CHALLENGE

Reengineering, re-strategizing, mergers, downsizing, quality efforts, and cultural renewal projects have become an integral part of business today in North America. Powerful flat-world economic forces are at work here, and these forces may grow even stronger over the next few decades. As a result, more and more organizations will be pushed to reduce costs, improve the quality of products and services, locate new opportunities for growth, and increase productivity.

Managers want to change the organization, overcoming obstacles to their vision, and that means overcoming inner vulnerabilities, adapting new skills, and adhering to new values. The challenge for business managers is to be a combination of warrior and prophet, delivering high performance in the business and being an advocate for their vision of the organization. Business has to continually change in small ways to stay competitive and may have to change drastically in response to external conditions.

The rate of change in the business world is not going to slow down anytime soon. If anything, competition in most industries will probably speed up even more over the next few decades. Enterprises everywhere will be presented with even more terrible hazards and wonderful opportunities, driven by the globalization of the economy along with related technological and social trends.

To date, major change efforts have helped some organizations adapt significantly to shifting conditions, have improved the competitive standing of others, and have positioned a few for a far better future. But in too many situations the improvements have been negligible and many organizations have failed to understand that change is essential. The options are either to grow or to shrink. They cannot afford to celebrate their achievements of the past and rest on their laurels. If they resist change the result would be wasted resources.

However, there is a downside to change and that downside, to some degree, is inevitable. Whenever we are forced to adjust to shifting conditions, pain is ever present. But a significant amount of the anguish we've witnessed in the past is avoidable.

For example, managers, in the past, have tried to change organizations without establishing a high enough sense of urgency in fellow managers and employees. This mistake is profound because change efforts always fail to achieve their objectives when urgency levels are low according to John Kotter of Harvard Business School.

A higher rate of urgency does not imply panic, anxiety or fear. It means a state in which complacency is virtually absent, in which people are always looking for both problems and opportunities, and in which the mantra is "action now."

Many times the person with the initial idea for

change has not been able to get the top 10, 15 people in the organization to support and pull together for his idea from the start. This group rarely includes all of the most senior people because some of them just won't buy in, at least at first. A lot of the top people are used to a certain way of doing things and have a natural tendency to resist change. But in the most successful cases, the coalition is always powerful - in terms of information and expertise, reputations and relationships, and the capacity for management. Individuals alone, no matter how competent or dynamic, never have all the firepower needed to overcome tradition and inertia except in very small organizations.

Urgency and a strong team effort are necessary but insufficient conditions for major transformation. Of the remaining elements that are always found in successful transformations, none is more important than a clear vision of the future.

Vision plays a key role in producing useful change by helping to direct, align, and inspire actions on the part of large numbers of people. Without an appropriate vision, a transformation effort can easily dissolve into a list of confusing, incompatible, and time-consuming projects that go in the wrong direction or nowhere at all. People will not make the sacrifices necessary to make the change a reality, even if they are unhappy with the status quo, unless they think the potential benefits of change are attractive. Without credible communication, and a lot of it, employees' hearts and minds are never captured.

One point to remember is that real transformation takes time. Complex efforts to change strategies or restructure businesses risk losing momentum if there are no short-term goals to meet and celebrate. Most people won't go on the long journey unless they see evidence within six to eighteen months that the journey is producing expected results. Without short-term wins, too many employees give up or actively join the resistance.

Creating short-term wins is different from hoping for short-term wins. The latter is passive, the former is active. In a successful transformation, managers actively look for ways to obtain clear performance improvements, establish goals in the yearly planning system and reward the people involved with recognition, promotions or money at the achievement of these objectives.

Change sticks only when it becomes a part of the corporate culture when it permeates into the very bloodstream of the work unit or corporate body. Until new behaviors are rooted in the social norms and shared values, they are always subject to being put on the back burner as soon as the focus shifts a little bit and that initial enthusiasm fades.

Two factors are particularly important in anchoring new approaches in an organization's culture. The first is a conscious attempt to exhibit clearly to people how specific behaviors and attitudes have helped improve performance. When people are left on their own to make the connections, as is often the case, they can easily misinterpret the cause and effect.

All organizations have unneeded internal interconnections between people and groups. The French subsidiary can't agree to anything without checking with corporate. The controller's department in the head office sends a ton of reports per week to the plants, where it is largely ignored. Because of some problem back in 2002, a routine was created in which salesmen make certain presentations to the marketing and manufacturing people, meetings that still go on today despite the existence of information technology that can communicate the same information more quickly and easily. In some firms this useless interdependence is overwhelming and makes major transformation more complex than it needs to be.

Establishing a need for Transformation

You have to increase the level of intensity if you want to stimulate those you want to change. Making the organization appreciate and acknowledge the need for change is one of the first and most important steps of any major organizational change.

The natural tendency of people is to stick with what they know and given a choice they would stick with the familiar, no matter how unproductive the outcome is. You have to demand change. You have to make it mandatory. And it is not enough to push just a few people to feel and face the pressures of change. A majority of your employees and virtually all of the top executives must be totally convinced that change is essential if you are to accomplish profound change.

No wonder successful change is such an uphill climb and so rarely occurs. You can't even get started on the road to major change until you invent or admit to a circumstance dire enough to raise the level of urgency.

Before you start climbing the ladder make sure it is leaning against the right wall. John Kotter predicts that "without an appropriate vision, a transformation effort can easily dissolve into a list of confusing, incompatible, and time-consuming projects that go in the wrong direction or nowhere at all."

The wisdom offered by increasing number of re-engineering specialists today is that large-scale complex change may be easier to accomplish than small-scale, incremental change. James Champy argues that when you face large-scale change, you're forced to confront the larger issues of culture and management style that exist in every organization. These issues of culture and style frequently make incremental change almost impossible to accomplish.

Just as entrepreneurial companies must deal with growth to achieve the necessary stale, older companies must move quickly to shed the antiquated practices that hobble them. Old structures and processes that hinder achievement of the new vision must be torn down and new ones that foster it must be built.

Roadblocks to Change

In a slow-moving world, all an organization needed was a good executive in charge. Teamwork at the top was not essential. However, in a moderately paced context, teamwork is necessary to deal with periodic changes, but much of the time the old model will still work. However, in the fast-moving world of today, teamwork is always enormously helpful if not imperative.

In an environment of constant change one individual won't have enough expertise to absorb rapidly shifting competitor, customer, and technological information. He won't have enough time to communicate all the important decisions to others. He will rarely have the dynamism or skills to single handedly gain commitments to change from large numbers of people.

Besides the challenges inherent in dealing with transformation, there are some other serious problems that arise for older companies out of having too much experience, and for younger ones from not having enough. These are attitudinal problems that are particularly precarious because the sufferers are often not aware that there is any problem. While wading through the eerie waters of transformation managers must also be vigilant about not creating an environment that is negative.

In established companies, decades of success result in the development of certain behaviors. When an organization has been successful, the driving mantra within it often is to stick to what has worked in the past. In these cases, being flexible and sensitive to his demands and serving the customer becomes an afterthought.

One of the biggest advantages that start-ups enjoy over most established companies is that they have flexibility. Because they are so new, small and nimble they don't have the layers of bureaucratic walls that render the more established companies inflexible. The older companies need to learn from new ones how to quickly change directions and launch new businesses to keep up with technology and customer taste.

Workers in these older companies waste tremendous amounts of time and emotional energy protecting the interests of their own units and positioning themselves for the next step up the corporate ladder. And, while they are doing this, they lose sight of the relationships with the customers, and suppliers that would allow them to compete successfully in a fast-paced marketplace. This one factor alone opens the door for the start-ups to step in and develop huge new markets in the backyards of the established juggernauts.

Some of the attitudinal problems that characterize older organizations are Individual motivations of employees, their attitudes towards the customer, their belief that "if they were here before they will come back." Their belief that "we've been here forever, we will survive" is detrimental to the continued success of the organization.

Finding and hiring the right people and effectively putting them to work is imperative but building the organizational foundations and management hierarchy needed to support a large organization is important as well. Here again speed is a critical issue. Accentuating the challenge on the growth route is the fact that increasing size brings with it some of the problems that older companies face. Growth quickly creates bureaucracy and resistance to change. Thus, the entrepreneurs must learn to play out the essential steps required to implement meaningful transformation albeit at a much smaller scale, over and over again.

The managers of older companies need to learn from successful entrepreneurs how to build and maintain a smart and effective workforce in a world where workers think nothing of changing employers every couple of years. The entrepreneurs who survive the growth phase do so only by becoming very skilled at developing and deploying people. In the 21st Century, when brains, creativity and energy are a company's primary assets, this is critically important.

The cultural pitfalls, or bad attitudes, that occur in newer companies are often the flip side of the ones that plague older companies. They generally arise out of having the foundations, structure and checks and balances missing in the organization. They also can have too little respect for the past and might refuse to learn from other people's mistakes. Further, because the more established folks didn't come up with the new technologies or didn't come up with brilliant ways to use them, people in the upstart companies tend to arrogantly discard everything - the rules, the ideas, the practices - that the established folks have ingrained in their culture. A culture that looks down upon everything from the past is just as misguided as the one that is not prepared to change at all.

The two single quickest killers are lack of respect for customers and poor management. Being arrogant and taking customers for granted led to a serious backlash and the self-destruction of many dot-com businesses. Add to this inconsistent leadership that allows the other bad attitudes to persist, and failure is almost certain.

Short-term Vs. Long term

Transformations sometimes go off track because people simply don't take notice of quick performance improvements. More often the effort is undermined because managers don't systematically plan for the creation of short-term wins. And the complete transformation is such an extensive and time-consuming endeavor that constituents lose sight of the goal. People stick with the familiar solely because, as Keynes put it, we are all dead in the long-run.

Short-term wins don't come about as the result of a little luck. They aren't merely possibilities. Managers plan for short-term wins, organize accordingly and implement the plan to make things happen. They understand how important short-term wins are to the motivation of the constituents to stay the course. The desired effect is not to maximize short-term results at the expense of the future. The point is to make sure that visible results lend sufficient credibility to the transformation effort.

People don't create short-term wins in their plans because they are overwhelmed. Often the complacency levels are pretty high or the vision isn't clear. Or planning for short-term wins doesn't receive sufficient time or attention.

Sometimes people don't try very hard to produce these wins because they believe you can't produce major change and achieve short-term results. Many believe that life in organizations is a trade-off between the short run and the long run. In this belief system, you can focus on the long-term and take the hits now or you can do well now and throw the future to the wind. According to this line of thinking, undertaking a major change program means looking to the long term, which in turn means expecting short term results to be problematic.

Targeting short-term wins during a transformation effort does increase the pressures on people. The argument is sometimes made that these extra demands are inappropriate. "We've got enough going on," people say, without more burdens. Give us a break."

This way of thinking is not without some merit. But more often than not, it has been found that short-term pressure can be a useful way to keep up the urgency rate. A year or two into a major change program, with the end not still in sight, people naturally tend to let up. They begin to think: "If this is going to take four more years, a slide to four and a quarter won't hurt." But as soon as the urgency rate goes down, everything becomes much harder to accomplish. Minor tasks that were completed in a month suddenly take three times as long. Of course, pressure doesn't always produce urgency. The burden of producing short-term wins can create stress and exhaustion as well. In successful change efforts, executives link pressure to urgency through the constant articulation of vision and strategies. "This is what we are trying to do and this is why it is so important. Without these short-term wins, we could lose everything. All that we do for our customers, shareholders, employees, and communities becomes problematic. So we have got to produce these results." This kind of communication gives meaning to hardships and spurs people on. Twelve to thirty-six months into a major change effort, tired employees often need renewed motivation.

Another element that undermines the planning for necessary wins is a lack of commitment by key managers to the change process in the new organizations. Without enough good management the planning and organizing will not be sufficient. Without able management, inadequate thought is usually given to the whole question of quantifying results. So existing barometers for success either fail to record important performance improvements or underestimate their size. Sequencing of events doesn't get sufficient attention.

Resisting Again

Resistance to change never fully disappears. Even if you're successful in the early stages of a transformation, you often end up bruising the ego of the self-centered manager who is appalled when a change encroaches on his territory, or the micro focused engineer who can't understand why you want to spend so much time worrying about customers, or the finance executive who thinks empowering employees does not make sense. You can drive these people underground but instead of changing or leaving, they will often sit there waiting for an opportunity to make a comeback.

Reality Check: The dark side of change

Change is risky, so you need to do some contingency planning. Just because something is worth doing there is no guarantee it will be successful. At this juncture optimism and faith alone are no substitute for careful planning. Put the three together, however, and you have a chance of success.

Once you know how to deal with disaster, you don't need to worry about it. This is why riders are taught how to fall off horses. If you have no plan to deal with disaster, the thought of it may haunt you, and with good reason.

Business leaders need to manage two types of change:

'In system' changes relate to changes in processes, management styles, hiring policies, sales methods and target markets while the core business remains the same. Of System changes are more profound. Examples are mergers, takeovers, new markets, new products or having to reorganize in the face of market shifts. A leader must make sure that there is enough In System change to handle any Of System changes.

Change and Leadership style

Implied in the organizational changes is the need for a major shift in management thought and practice. Many companies and their managers are not changing with the times. For example, our society values democracy, yet most companies are governed by autocracy; our society values capitalism, but many companies practice feudalism. Motivational theory in the 21st century has shifted its organization from stomach to heart to mind.

In the 21st Century there has been a shift in the role of the manager from hero to developer, from commander to consultant, from 'boss' to mentor, from decision maker to value clarifier. The new manager is moving away from confrontational dialogue to empathic dialogue, from retaining power to sharing power, from adversarial relationships to collaborative relationships based on collaborative relationships based on mutual interests. However, my concern here is that the balance might tip a little too much. Managers might show weakness and camouflage it as kindness, a lack of resolve is sold as flexibility. These inconsistencies are fatal in the face of major transformation effort.

Questions to Ask

1) Is not changing an option for an organization?

2) Is smaller change easier to accomplish than huge change efforts?

3) Do you create a sense of urgency and prepare people for the pain of change?

4) Do you sell your vision of the change and get the team on board?

5) Do you establish the need for change within the organization?

6) Do you create a system of quantifiable short-term wins on the way to major change?

7) Are you cautious of resisters to the change effort even when the change effort is well on its way?

8) Do you get the key managers on board with the change effort?

9) Since change is risky do you do contingency planning when undertaking a transformation effort?

10) Do you make sure it becomes a part of the culture rather than something that would fizzle out over time?

The Management of Self

So far we have discussed managing others within a team. Even more challenging a situation than managing others in a period of difficulty might be the management of ones self. The management of self is critical. Without it, managers may do more harm than good. Like incompetent physicians, incompetent managers can make people sicker and less vital. Sometimes illnesses are caused by doctors and hospitals as side effects of medical intervention. Managers, too, can cause as well as cure problems. A certain degree of positive self regard is imperative. We learn the meaning of positive self regard from responses to the question: "Which are your major strengths and weaknesses?" For the most part, when leaders are asked this question they emphasize their strengths and tend to soft-pedal or minimize their weaknesses, which is not to say that they are not aware

Management's key objective is to stabilize all systems and accurately predict process results. Once stable and predictable, processes can be controlled and improved and variation reduced. Statistical analysis is the basic tool to understand, predict, and thus reduce variation in systems and their components. However, it is through knowledge of his own self that a good manager can develop that internal GPS to develop an understanding of his constituents and the challenge of the situation.

Deming says that 90 percent of all problems or defects are the result of the system rather than the individual. But people design, develop, and control all other elements of any system. The more people are unstable or subject to variable, unpredictable performance, the more unstable and subject to variation become the systems they design and implement. Anything management can do to stabilize the performance of people, empower them to become more consistent, more predictable, would have a dual benefit. The quality of products would also become more stable and more predictable. We must understand people, Deming says, their interaction with each other, and the systems in which they work and learn - their motivations, intrinsic and extrinsic.

The Importance of Self Awareness

Warren Bennis said that self-knowledge was an essential part of defining integrity. He observed that knowing oneself was the most difficult task any of us faced. He said "Until you truly know yourself, strengths and weaknesses, know what you want to do and why you want to do it, you cannot succeed in any but the most superficial sense of the word."

One's capacity to align words and deeds depends on how well one knows himself. The better one knows oneself, the better one can make sense of the often incomprehensible and conflicting messages one receives daily. Do this or that. We need internal guidance to navigate the permanent white waters of today's environment.

Inside Vs Outside

Lasting solutions to problems, lasting happiness and success, come from within. What results from the outside is unhappy people who feel victimized and immobilized, focused on all the weaknesses of other people and the circumstances they feel are responsible for their own stagnant condition.

The Within approach suggests that if we want to develop the trust that results in mutually acceptable agreements and synergistic solutions, we must control our own lives and subordinate short-term desires to higher purposes and principles. Private victories precede public victories. Making and keeping promises to ourselves precedes making and keeping promises to others. And it's a continuing process, an upward spiral of growth that leads to progressively higher forms of independence.

The deep, fundamental problems we face cannot be solved on the superficial level on which they were created. We need a new level of thinking - based on principles of effective management - to solve these deep concerns. We need a character-based "Within" approach.

Within means to start first with self - to start with the most inside part of self - with your paradigms, your character, and your motives. If you want to have more freedom, more latitude in your job, be a more responsible, helpful, contributing employee. If you want to be trusted be trustworthy.

The primary source of continuing problems in many companies and cultures has been the dominant social paradigm of outward focus. Everyone is convinced that the problem is out there and if others would shape up or suddenly ship out of existence, the problem would be solved.

The principles of effectiveness are deeply scripted within us, in our conscience and in our quiet reflection on life experience. To recognize and develop them and to use them in meeting our deepest concerns, we need to think differently, to shift our paradigm to a new, deeper, level.

The key to working from the within, the paradigm of primary greatness, is to educate and obey the conscience - that unique human endowment that senses congruence or disparity with correct principles and lifts us towards them.

Just as the education of nerve and sinew is vital to the athlete and education of the mind is vital to the scholar, education of the conscience is vital to the good manager. Training the conscience, however, requires even more discipline. It requires honest living, reading inspiring literature and thinking noble thoughts. Just as junk food and lack of exercise can ruin an athlete's condition, things that are obscene or crude can breed an inner darkness that numbs our highest sensibilities and substitutes the social conscience of "Will I be found out?" for the natural conscience of "What is right or wrong?"

Good managers have a sense of stewardship about everything in life, including their time, talents, money, possessions, relationships, family and even their bodies.

They recognize the need to use all their resources for positive purposes and they expect to be held accountable.

Good managers return kindness for offense, patience for impatience. They bring out the best in those around them by seeking to bless when being cursed, to go the extra mile, to forgive and forget, to move on in life with cheerfulness, believing in the potential goodness of people and the eventual triumph of truth.

Gandhi said "First they ignore you, then they ridicule you, then they attack you, and then you win."

The moment a person attempts to become his own advocate, seeking to defend or justify himself or to return in kind the treatment he receives, he becomes caught up in exchange of negative energy. He and his enemy are then on the same turf, and they will either fight or flee in such destructive ways as manipulation, violence, withdrawal, indifference, litigation, or political battles.

"I know who I was, who I am, and where I want to be," says Dan Kaplan, president of Hertz Equipment Rental Corporation. "So in other words, I know the level of commitment that I am prepared to make and why I am prepared to make that level of commitment personally. I know what it takes to achieve success for me. That success for me comes from paying a big price, putting a lot of work and a lot of sacrifice behind it."

To know genuinely the level of commitment you are willing to make, you must discover three essential aspects of yourself: your competencies, your values and your confidence. Your values, your personal credo, give you the right words to say. Your capabilities, your competencies, give you the skills to turn your words into actions. And your trust in your abilities to do what you believe, your confidence, gives you the will to make use of those skills.

Self Confidence: Believing you can do it

Self-confidence is not the same as competence, of course. Knowing that you have the competence and believing that in a given situation you can use your skills to achieve your goals are different mental sets. Bandura observes that "a capability is only as good as its execution. People often fail to perform optimally because they doubt their ability to put those skills to use in a particular situation. It is thus not only competence that determines execution and outcome. Belief in one's abilities counts.'

Beliefs about one's capabilities influence personal motivation. They determine how much effort a person is likely to exert and how long the individual will persevere when the task gets difficult. The greater the self-efficacy, the less stress and depression people feel in taxing and threatening situations. The greater the belief in their own capabilities the higher the goals people set for themselves and the firmer they are in commitment to them. And self-efficacy even has the power to influence career choices. Bendura explains, "The more efficacious people judge themselves to be, the wider the range of career options they consider appropriate and the better they prepare themselves educationally for different pursuits."

From this research, you can see that self-belief in efficacy influences the management roles you might select. If you believe a particular management task is outside of your control or will require more time and energy than you can muster, you are unlikely to pursue the task – even if you know that it is essential to your group's success. Belief in your own efficacy influences the level of challenge you will seek.

In many management development programs an activity requires people to walk across a five-inch-wide beam. When the beam is placed on the ground everyone confidently scampers across. No problem. But when asked to climb a rope ladder and then walk a six-inch-wide beam that is thirty feet off the ground, people react quite differently. Some say, "not in a million years" or "you must be kidding." And then there are those who race across without giving it a second thought.

Managers need to understand their limitations as well as their strengths. Of course, managers do not have to give in to their limitations; they do not have to accept them as permanent. In fact, there is no way anyone can overcome a doubt unless it is confronted and unless the competence and confidence are developed to handle a similar encounter in the future. But managers must not experiment with constituents as subjects. They should have well founded confidence in their skills before involving others.

It may be easier to say what positive self-regard isn't than what it is. To begin with, it is not crowing self-importance or egoistic self-centeredness that we have in mind. Nor is it what's ordinarily meant by a "narcissistic character." There is no trace of self-worship or cockiness in good managers.

But they know their worth. They trust themselves without letting their egos or images get in the way. One manager put it in terms of self-respect. She said,

'To have self-respect is everything. Without it, we are nothing but unwilling slaves, at everybody's mercy, especially those we fear or hold in contempt…. You think, "Well, no job is good enough; after all, if they want me, hired me, how could they be any good?" Groucho Marx's greatest line says it all for those without self-respect, "I wouldn't join any club that would have me as a member." They choke on self-reproach. For them, every encounter demands too much and receives too little becomes a monument to their own sloth, an epitaph to their guilt. Without self-respect, we give ourselves away and make the ultimate sacrifice: sell ourselves out!'

Recognizing strengths and compensating for weaknesses represent the first step in achieving positive self-regard. The second element in positive self-regard is the nurturing of skills with discipline – that is to keep working on and developing ones talents. The capacity to develop and improve their skills distinguished good managers from followers. They seemed to be responsible for their own evolution and even could appropriately be called "self-evolvers."

While there is no substitute for achievement managers need not be exceptional in every way. But limitations cannot be ignored. A trait that begins as little more than a personal hang up can become tragic through repetition, so effective managers learn to compensate for their imperfections before they become perilous.

To sum up what I mean by positive self-regard. It consists of three major components: knowledge of one's strengths, the capacity to nurture and develop those strengths and the ability to discern the fit between one's strengths and weaknesses and the organization's needs. Another way of thinking about positive self-regard as it specifically relates to work and jobs is that individuals who possess it are good at their jobs and have the requisite skills. They enjoy their work it satisfies their basic needs and motives. And, finally, they are proud of their work; it reflects their value system.

In the case of managers I observed that they used four key skills. Firstly, they have the capacity to approach problems in terms of the present rather than the past. Secondly, they have the ability to treat those who are close to them with the same courteous attention that they extend to strangers and casual acquaintances. Thirdly, they have the ability to trust others, even if the risk seems great. And fourth, they have the ability to do without constant approval and recognition from others.

Criticism is a frequent by-product of significant undertakings. It tests the foundations of positive self-regard as does nothing else. And the more valid the criticism the more difficult it is to receive it.

The imperative in organizational management is that the manager's style pulls rather than pushes people on. This style of influence works by attracting and energizing people to an exciting vision of what might be. It motivates by identification with the future. The good manager articulates and embodies the ideals toward which the organization is striving. This vision of that ideal feels attainable and enrolls the constituents.

"Self" and Leadership

It seems perfectly obvious that one can learn to lead. After all, nearly three fourths of North American companies send people to leadership classes every year. Practically every business school offers executive education to teach leadership theory. Of course one can learn to lead.

If one ask the people who are teaching most of the leadership courses – whether they think leadership can be taught, one will probably get an interesting response. For every Warren Bennis who maintains that no one can teach leadership…. Leadership is character and judgment (and) two things that you can't teach are character and judgment," you can encounter a Peter Drucker who states flatly that "leadership must be learned and can be learned."

Most leadership scholars think your leadership potential is helped along if you are born with reasonably good mental and physical capacities and have early childhood experiences that put the leadership fire in your belly. Some early childhood challenges and hardship that don't substantially undermine your self-esteem are helpful. Just as the moth gains strength by having the challenge of tearing through its cocoon so would you as you grow and develop into a leader.

Some scholars want potential leaders to have an education that goes beyond the subjects, such as marketing, finance, and information systems, that form the backbone courses of most business schools. Lee Bolman and Terence Deal, coauthors of Leading with Soul: An Uncommon Journey of Spirit prefer to have potential leaders steep themselves in poetry, literature, music and art. John Gardner takes this idea further by suggesting that would-be leaders should be exposed to "the whole range of liberal arts."

The scale measure pervades a lot of discussions about success. The more constituents you have, the better at managing you must be. The argument is easy to understand. It takes extraordinary talent and energy to manage a large company, country, or movement, particularly over time. Outstanding skills are necessary. Certainly there is a level of superior competence involved.

But taken to its logical extreme, no leader could be judged entirely successful, even those who have influenced millions. Judaism, Islam, Buddhism, and Christianity, for example have thrived for centuries. Moses, Mohammed, Siddhartha Gautama, and Christ are considered by many to be extraordinary leaders. But in their lifetimes, they did not convert every soul to their beliefs. Not everyone has been converted to this day.

Or take another person on the list of most-admired leaders, Mother Teresa. Her ceaseless compassionate work on behalf of the poor around the world has won her a Noble Prize. Yet she has very few constituents by comparison to many corporate presidents. Does that mean she is not as good a leader as they are?

These issues of scope reflect values. If we value bigger, more grand, and longer, then we are likely to be disappointed in most leaders and in ourselves and to limit to a very few the number of people who can lead. In my view, leadership is both local and global. Acts of credible leadership come in all sizes. You can lead people to change the world, or you can lead yourself to change your own work space. Leadership is also transitory, and most often lasts for only a relatively short time. There are those whose influence has spanned centuries and crossed continents, but they are not the only ones who have led. Those whose influence has spanned only a few days and a few blocks can still have taken people to places they have never been before

The Discipline Challenge

Anyone who does what she must only when she is in the mood to do it or when it is convenient for her isn't going to be successful nor will people respect her. If one can determine what's really important and release oneself from everything else, it's a lot easier to follow through on what's important.

To develop a lifestyle of discipline, one of the first

tasks must be to challenge and eliminate any tendency to make excuses. As French classical writer Francois La Rochfoucauld said, "Almost all our faults are more pardonable than the methods we think up to hide them." If you have several reasons why you can't be self-disciplined, realize that they are really just a bunch of excuses - all of which need to be challenged if you want to go to the next level as a manager.

Anytime you concentrate on the difficulty of the work instead of its results or rewards, you're likely to become discouraged. Dwell on it too long, and you'll develop self-pity instead of self-discipline. The next time you're facing a must-do task and you're thinking of doing what's convenient instead of paying the price, change your focus. Count the benefits of doing what's right, and then dive in.

Our Strengths - and our Weaknesses

Defensiveness takes many forms: minimizing the facts, filtering out crucial information, rationalizations and "good excuses"-anything to rob the facts of their emotional truth. And people around us may tend to collude with our denial. Among the more difficult kinds of information to get in organizational life is honest, constructive feedback about how we are doing, especially about our lapses. Coworkers, subordinates, and bosses have an easier time complaining to each other out of earshot of a person than having an honest and open talk with that person about what's wrong. There is a Faustian bargain in this collusion to act as though everything is fine when in fact it is not, for we buy the illusion of harmony and effectiveness at the cost of the truth that could open the way to genuine improvement.

Following are some of the personality-based blind spots that appear in managers at all levels as pointed out in a study done by Robert Kaplan:

Blind ambition: Has to win or appear "right" at all costs; competes instead of cooperates; exaggerates his or her own value and contribution; is boastful and arrogant; sees people in black-and-white terms as allies or enemies.

Unrealistic goals: Sets overly ambitious, unattainable goals for the group or organization; is unrealistic about what it takes to get jobs done.

Relentless striving: Compulsively hardworking at the expense of all else in life; runs on empty; is vulnerable to burn out.

Driving others: Pushing other people too hard, burning them out; micromanages and takes over instead of delegating; comes across as abrasive or ruthless and insensitive to the emotional harm to others.

Power hungry: Seeks power for his or her own interests, rather than the organization's; pushes a personal agenda regardless of other perspectives; is exploitative.

Insatiable need for recognition: Addicted to glory; takes credit for others' efforts and puts blame on them for mistakes; sacrifices follow-through in pursuit of the next victory.

Preoccupation with appearances: Needs to look good

at all costs; is overly concerned with public image; craves the material trappings of prestige.

Need to seem perfect: Enraged by or rejects criticism, even if realistic; blames others for his or her failures; cannot admit mistakes or personal weaknesses.

Such blind spots can actually motivate people to avoid self-awareness, since by knowing themselves they would have to admit to failings they cannot bear to acknowledge. This need to deny makes such people resistant to any and all feedback-and can make them a nightmare to work with and for.

Some managers have only a rosy view of themselves - if they rated themselves significantly better on abilities such as being considerate and flexible, trustworthy and credible. At the extreme, this is the self-view of the narcissist, who admits no flaws, exaggerates his own abilities, and dodges feedback, not wanting to hear about any deficiencies.

Superior performers intentionally seek feedback; they want to hear how others perceive them, realizing that this is valuable information. That may be part of the reason people who are self-aware are superior performers.

Character

Those who are clear about their values and beliefs have laid the cornerstones for a firm ethical structure. People who have developed the skills to enact their beliefs possess the moral capacity to achieve good ends with good means. People who have faith in their abilities to execute effectively and consistently even under duress and challenge display moral fortitude. The quest for character is a noble one, though often baffling and frustrating. Just when we think we have grasped its nature, it evades us. Yet if we wish to be judged by the content of our character, we must decide what content we wish it to consist of.

Audit your ability to succeed

If you want to continue to be of worth to your clients, you have to stay current with the problems that are of interest to them. Your credo provides you with a good starting place but you must also identify the specific job related competencies you need to master to lead your constituents.

How do your abilities compare to what the situation, role, and tasks call for? How well can you execute what you say you value? Where are the gaps? What specific knowledge and abilities do you have that will enable you to succeed in this environment? Which must you acquire? What experiences do you need to sharpen these competencies? Who is the very best in your field, and how do you compare to that person? What can you do to become the best? Would your constituents respond to these questions in the same way?

Questions to Ask

1) Do you know what you want to do?

2) Do you know what your strengths and limitations are?

3) How would you achieve happiness?

4) What do you do when someone is offensive and impatient with you?

5) Do you continue to believe in yourself in the face of continued adversity? On a scale of 1 to 10?

6) Do you have the ability to take people as they are and not as you would like them to be?

7) Can you do without constant approval of others?

8) Do you make excuses for failure?

9) Do you stick with your values in times of adversity?

Bibliography

The structure and dynamics of organizations and groups,
Bernie, Eric.
New York, Grove Press (1963)

The seven habits of highly effective people: restoring the
character ethic
By Covey, Stephen R.
New York: Simon and Schuster, 1990, c1989

The visionary leader : from mission statement to a
thriving organization, here's your blueprint for building
an inspired, cohesive, customer-oriented team
By Wall, Bob
Rocklin, Calif. Prima Pub., c1992

Principle-centered leadership
By Covey, Stephen R.
New York; Toronto: Summit Books, c1991

Visionary leadership: creating a compelling sense of direction for your organization
By Nanus, Burt
San Francisco: Jossey-Bass, c1992

The leader in you: how to win friends, influence people, and succeed in a changing world
By Levine, Stuart R.
New York: Simon and Schuster, 1993

Reengineering management: the mandate for new leadership: managing the change of the reengineered corporation
By Champy, James
New York: HarperBusiness, c1995.

Pathways to performance: a guide to transforming yourself, your team, and your organization
By Clemmer, Jim
Toronto: Macmillan Canada, 1995

Leading minds: an anatomy of leadership
By Gardner, Howard
New York, NY: BasicBooks, c1995.

Credibility: how leaders gain and lose it, why people demand it
By Kouzes, James M.,
San Francisco: Jossey-Bass Publishers, c1993

Executive Leadership: a practical guide to managing complexity
By Jaques, Elliott

Falls Church, VA: Cason Hall; Cambridge, Mass.:
Blackwell Business, 1991.

Leading Change
By Kotter, John P.,
Boston, Mass. Harvard Business School Press, c1996.

Developing the leaders around you
By Maxwell, John C.,
Nashville, Tenn.: T. Nelson, c 1996

The leadership engine : how winning companies build
leaders at every level
By Tichy, Noel M.
New York: Harper Business, 1997

The guru guide: the best ideas of the top management
thinkers
By Boyett, Joseph H
New York: Wiley, 1998.

Leaders: strategies for taking charge
By Bennis, Warren G. 1997
New York: Harper Business, 1997.

Learning to lead: a workbook on becoming a leader
By Bennis, Warren G.
Reading, Mass.: perseus Books,1997.

Gifts of leadership: a guidebook for visionaries with their
feet on the ground
By Hendricks, Gay
Toronto: Bantam Books, 1997.

How to think like a CEO: the 22 vital traits you need to be the person at the top
By Benton, D. A.
New York: Warner Books, c1996.

The leader's change handbook: an essential guide to setting direction and taking action
By Conger, Jay A.
San Francisco: Jossey-Bass, c1999

The leader's handbook: making things happen, getting things done
By Scholtes, Peter R.
New York: McGraw Hill, c1998

The Leader of the Future
By The Drucker Foundation
San Francisco: Jossey-Bass, c1996

Co-Leaders: the power of great partnerships
By Heenan, D.A.
New York: John Wiley and Sons, c1999

A briefing for leaders: Communication as the ultimate exercise of power
By Dilenschneider, R.L.
New York: Harper Business, c1992

Leading from the heart: choosing courage over fear in the workplace
By Gilley, K.
Boston: Butterworth-Heinemann, c 1997

The future of leadership: today's top leadership thinkers speak to tomorrow's leaders
By Bennis W.
San Francisco: Josey Bass, c 2001

The Balanced Scorecard: Translating Strategy into Action (Hardcover)
by <u>Robert S. Kaplan</u> (Author), <u>David P. Norton</u> (Author)
1992